MW00477813

TRIED & *(STILL)* TRUE

Also by Erik Tyler

The Best Advice So Far

and coming soon

You Always Have A Choice

TRIED & (*Still*) TRUE

ERIK TYLER

Cover design: Erik Tyler

"Frog on a Penny Farthing" (& bugs!) Illustrations:
Michael Phipps

For booking information:
booking@TheBestAdviceSoFar.com

1st Edition
USA

For my mother, Barbara,
for preserving an invaluable family legacy through story,
and for exemplifying both wisdom and humility
with your own life story.

contents

thanks & acknowledgements

**Appreciation is a wonderful thing:
It makes what is excellent in others
belong to us as well.** *—Voltaire*

Mom — In addition to the book's dedication, your ability to laugh, rain or shine, and to listen like it matters have infused this book. (After all, you were quite literally sitting beside me for a good deal of the writing of it—Florida!)

Nana and Grampa Kwiatkowski — You lived well, you live on in me, and your story is still being told. I miss you both more than I can say. (Cuckoo for you!)

Sean — Our ongoing conversations about the craft of writing—and of living—have inspired me and stirred me to action often. You continually remind me that a guy and his words can be both smart and down to earth.

Jed — During the dark stretches when it seemed this book might never see the light, your willingness to lend some of your enthusiasm, to ask thoughtful "what if…?" questions, and to dream out loud together made a world of difference.

Diana — No matter what life brings, you always manage to send the perfect note at the perfect time, infused with care, honesty and cheer. Watching you as a writer continue to set and pursue new goals regularly while being open about the struggles and obstacles you face has been an ongoing source of encouragement and motivation for me.

Chad — For pushing me, for sending well-timed texts, for sharing what you see from your place on the road, for providing a swell retreat and for being ridiculous as needed—thank you.

Dib — No one else I know can say so much with so few words. How you turn a raise of eyebrow or a shift in tone into hope is some sort of voodoo, I'm sure of it. For *everything*, well…"you know."

Kathy — For your fine-toothed comb and your enormous heart.

William — Your willingness to listen to every word of this book (often more than once), to be vulnerable enough to laugh out loud or cringe or cry at all the right parts, to offer unfiltered feedback and to keep me pointed toward the finish line when I couldn't see it have all been indispensible. Oh, and… *microsculptimals*!

Thank you to each person who has listened to or read my words, and who has been willing to share with me your own story in the process. You are constant reminders of why I do what I do.

Finally, as strange as it may seem from this side of the book, I'd also like to acknowledge and thank the many thinkers and writers from across the centuries and around the world, who devoted countless hours of toil and passion so that wisdom could be preserved beyond your lifetime and passed on to each new generation. Though you may be gone, you are not forgotten.

TRIED & *(STILL)* TRUE

**I've learned
that I still have a lot to learn.**

Maya Angelou

introduction

TWENTY-FIRST CENTURY AMERICANS are obsessed with *new*.

While Notre Dame has stood proudly in Paris for more than eight centuries—drawing as many as 50,000 visitors from around the world daily—we in the States seem all too quick to bulldoze our history in favor of gleaming office buildings and freshly paved strip malls, losing irreplaceable treasures in the process.

From seasonal fashions to smart phones, cars to careers, religion to relationships, we've become conditioned to believe—to accept as fact—that *old* is inherently bad while *new* is not only good, but *necessary*. Even "old" body parts are subject to being replaced with newer, younger ones.

I completed my last book, *The Best Advice So Far*, exactly one year to the day after I'd started. I still remember typing the period after the last word of the last sentence of the last chapter. It was exactly 3:18 AM. I was so into what I'd been writing that, when my fingers finally stopped typing, it was a good minute or two before the realization set in: *I just finished the book*. I didn't know what one should feel or do on such an occasion. All I could think to do was to drive to the all-night convenience store, buy a Nestlé Quik strawberry milk and drink it in the aisle, as a sort of toast to the occasion.

There was a sudden flurry of activity around the e-book release. Reactions were overwhelmingly positive, including endorsements from a *New York Times* best-selling author and a vice president from Google. Even the title itself was based on exclamations from a lifetime of mentoring that had led to that point: "Thank you! I never would have thought to try what you suggested. It really was *the best advice* I've gotten!"

It was a rush. It all felt so… *new.*

I'll never forget receiving the first print copy about a year later. The anticipation of opening the box. The heft of it. Even the smell. Again, it was the beginning of a new adventure.

Any author will tell you that we succumb just as easily to the lure of *new.* There's nothing quite like the feeling of having a *new* release. Conversely, if we're being honest, there's a sort of—how to say it?—*tarnished* feeling, as the gap between the copyright date and the one on the current calendar widens. That is, in simplest terms, *old* to a writer begins to feel synonymous with *bad.*

And yet the words and thoughts and stories inside *haven't changed.*

Our collective addiction to *new* has us continually scrambling to read the latest releases by hip, young motivational writers who promise to reveal their "five secrets" and never-before-heard solutions to our problems—all neatly packaged in slick and impressive sounding buzzwords.

I went to great pains with *The Best Advice So Far* to point out—across social media, on my blog and inside the book itself—that I take no credit for having *invented* the advice in that book. While the book was new, the ideas it contained were *not.*

In that respect, even from its first day out in the world, the book was very *old*.

Let me suggest here, as I did at the start of *The Best Advice So Far*, that if something is true—if it *works*—then it's *always* been true. The best anyone can do is pay attention, discover it, put it into practice, and pass it along to others.

Put another way, while language and culture may change with time, wisdom itself is *old*.

Timeless.

That is all to say, our grandmothers and great-great-grandpappies (all of whom, mind you, were young and quite hip in their day) … *knew stuff*.

Important stuff.

They were smart people. Tenacious. Resourceful.

And despite their not having had laser teeth whitening or social media followings or audiences of thousands paying $500 a head to attend conferences in order to hear what they had to say, they'd learned a thing or two about what *really matters*.

How to live at peace in a war-torn world.

How to stretch a dollar during the worst of times.

How to navigate conflict and to be a good neighbor.

How to have character in the face of trials.

How to be truly happy, come what may.

To modern ears, the speech these old souls used may sound quaint, outdated—even archaic. Yet the principles for living remain every bit as powerful as they ever were.

It is my hope, within the pages that follow, to blow the dust off some moldering maxims from yesteryear, to give them a good spit-shine, and to introduce a new generation of discerning thinkers to the inimitable insights, sheer brilliance and just plain common sense captured by these **tried-and-(*still*)-true** gems of practical wisdom.

what to expect

THROUGHOUT THIS BOOK, I use stylistic conventions that do not strictly adhere to the standard rules of grammar and mechanics (for instance, my chapter titles are all in lowercase, and I use frequent sentence fragments). I trust this won't upset the apple carts of any English language purists. I assure you, I'm a flag-waving, card-carrying grammar nerd; and yet my approach to writing has always been guided by two superseding "rules": 1.) know the rules so that you can break them *on purpose* rather than willy-nilly; and 2.) where proper grammar would inhibit mood, intent, personal impact or clarity of message, allowances must be made.

Regarding layout, each chapter of this book is organized into six parts, and it will be helpful for you to understand what to expect from each of these distinct sections at the outset.

The opening of each chapter, which is unlabeled, contains an observation or story that serves as a lead-in to the central proverb for that chapter. It's intended to provide real-world context and personal connection to a topic, before revealing too much more about the proverb itself.

The remaining four subheadings are drawn from parts of the book title. I'll list each of those subheadings on the following page, along with a brief description of its purpose.

Finally, each chapter ends with a section called "Questions & A Challenge," which I've included to provide you or your group further opportunity for discussion and application.

TRIED

chapter proverb introduced

In this section, I give a history of the proverb and how it came into English. I then say a good deal about the lives of the people to whom credit should be given for the survival of the proverb to our day. My intention isn't merely to talk about origins, but to help the reader connect with these writers and to see that they weren't dusty old men sequestered away in molding libraries; rather, they were young, modern (for their time), *real* people, living full and interesting and complex lives, just like you and I.

...&...

This section may contain fun facts, trivia or tangentially related points of interest. As the subheading suggests, this information is literarily secondary to the main points. So don't rack your brain trying to pull all the pieces together into a linear flow. Just take it at face value (and then enjoy how cool you'll seem at parties when you casually bring up what you learn here).

(Still) **TRUE**

This section is all about application: putting feet to the proverb in everyday life. To that end, you'll find anecdotes, examples, personal challenges—and plenty more stories.

Not **TRUE**

The closing section is included for the sake of hammering out what the proverb *doesn't* mean. It's an extension of the "*(Still)* **TRUE**" section; and yet it's unique in that it's designed to expel common misconceptions, prevent misinterpretation or remove excuses or other barriers that might otherwise prevent the reader from experiencing the full benefits of using the wisdom in real-world situations.

Questions **&** *A Challenge*

Here, you'll find questions for group discussion or self-reflection, along with a personal challenge related to the chapter.

1

know

NTIL MODERN TIMES, written wisdom was rare. It had a weight to it, an *otherness*. And so it was approached with a kind of reverence.

The earliest human writing—cuneiform dating back to before 3000 B.C.—was etched into clay tablets or stone. I wasn't there, but I'm guessing that, given the sheer work involved, those ancient Mesopotamians weren't breaking out the chisel every time they saw a goat do something they thought was cute.

Not long after, papyrus and parchment came along; yet even as something akin to modern paper finally hit the scene around 100 B.C., it was still regarded as precious. And writing was an uncommon skill, as was reading.

Thus, over the course of nearly five millennia, one will notice a distinct absence of Sunday funnies. Likewise, as far as we know, not a single scribe of old was beckoned to jot down celebrity gossip.

Like paper, ink was a valuable resource. There were no erasers. Putting words in print, therefore, was a solemn undertaking—one prefaced by days of contemplation, reflection and much mental editing before a quill was ever dipped. It was called *committing* one's thoughts to writing because it did, indeed, require a commitment.

Consequently, the things people wrote down *mattered*, both to writer and reader (or, more often, listener) alike.

Even after the printing press made mass publication

possible, notable quotes continued to be etched into the architecture, as if to say, "This is enduring wisdom. Pay heed. Remember."

The Library of Congress, established in 1800, is adorned with many such quotes using Latin fonts depicting "U" in its early "V"-like form, including this one by sixteenth-century poet Sir Philip Sidney:

"THEY ARE NEVER ALONE THAT ARE ACCOMPANIED WITH NOBLE THOVGHTS."

I saw an intriguing Sondheim performance at the nearby Huntington Theater. Built in 1925—which is relatively recent in the scope of things—it too bears gilded lettering above the stage, a quote from Shakespeare's *Hamlet*:

"TO HOLD AS 'TWERE THE MIRROR UP TO NATURE"

By the early 1990s, as I was finishing college, wisdom and inspiration were still largely the stuff of books or plaques. However, statements of self-expression or inspiration had also been adorning walls since the late 1960s in the form of posters. Still, even these were an *investment*. You went to specific stores to find them. You spent time flipping through scores of designs in hard plastic protectors hanging from sliding racks— *clack, clack, clack*. And they weren't cheap. So unless you found one that *perfectly* aligned with your particular aesthetic and credo, you most often left empty-handed.

Then, there was also the matter of wall space. Often, putting up a *new* poster meant deciding, with a mix of angst and nostalgia, which existing favorite would first need to be retired. This is all to say that, given the cost to the owner in terms of money, time and thought—the words printed on posters still *meant something*.

Not so any longer.

The twenty-first century stands in stark contrast with the entirety of written history that came before. From cafes, couches and cars, fingers or thumbs fly across keypads to indulge our every whim where words are concerned.

"Line at Lucky's = so long… zzzz"

"I just saw a mangy squirrel!"

"Peanut butter! Yum!"

If only the prolific proclamations were all so innocuous. Alas, we've also become comfortable with publishing just about *everything*—

however fleeting or trifling,

however ill-informed or ill-crafted,

however hateful or hurtful,

however careless or tactless,

however argumentative or condescending or simply inane—all without a moment's hesitation.

Of course, it's not all bad. There's lots of good in the mix as well.

Lots and lots.

I myself have been blogging since 2011, trying along with many other bloggers out there to make a positive difference in people's lives using every available means. Yet do you know how many blogs there are across the world as I'm writing this page? Go ahead, take a guess.

The first blog post was published in 1994. Here, a mere 25 years later, the best estimate is that there are nearly half a billion blogs on the web.

Half a billion.

And that is blog *sites,* not *posts.* WordPress alone estimates that nearly 80 million blog posts per month are published   using its platform.

Add to this the never-ending stream of inspirational quotes—memes set against gorgeously photographed backdrops—scrolling up our screens.

And yet, how often do we actually stop to ponder the implications or applications they tout?

Scroll, scroll, scroll.

Like, Like, Like.

Share. Retweet. Repeat.

When you really think about it, the fact that you just read the last three lines and *understood them at all...* well, it says something. Because prior to the latter half of the 2000s, those words would have been construed as utter gibberish.

I guess what I'm trying to say is that we've got access to more words than ever before. *And yet they mean continually less.*

It's a perpetual rain of inspiration, yet we collectively die of thirst for lack of drinking any of it in.

Let me offer one more analogy. Imagine yourself pushing your shopping cart up and down the grocery store aisles, surveying all of the food. You smell the fresh basil and thyme. You press your nose against the deli glass, admiring the wares on the other side. You smack your lips as you pass by the peanut butter. You ogle the oranges.

You pinch the peaches and point at the peppers, oohing and aahing and exclaiming how much you *like* them.

But you don't buy anything.

You don't eat any of it.

You don't digest it.

You don't let it *become a part of you.*

I ask you: *What good would all the admiration do you?*

The same holds true with knowledge and *potentially* life-changing wisdom or advice. Agreement alone isn't enough. Pressing "Like" is fine; but if there's no act of intention to integrate into your life what you read or hear, it's like that inspirational trip to the grocery store. Unless you eventually pick some of it up and take it home and eat it, you'll starve.

The thing is, truth isn't any less true now than it ever was. Wisdom hasn't become any less wise. What's more, the intrinsic power of words to provoke choice and change—both in ourselves and in the world—is no less powerful today than at any point in history.

In other words, the problem isn't the words. The problem is *our relationship with them.*

And that is precisely why I set about to write *Tried & (Still) True.*

TRIED

Know thyself.

If I'm going to be offering a compilation of noteworthy written wisdom, we may as well begin at the beginning.

Many people attribute "Know thyself" to Socrates. Truth is, no one knows for sure just when the saying came about or who should be credited with having said it first, though most scholars seem to agree that it hails from as far back as Ancient Egypt.

One thing's for sure: it's *old*.

And it certainly sounds plenty *deep* as well, evoking images of some robe-clad and wizened sage speaking in hushed tones to eager neophytes.

Moreover, *something* about this age-old advice has caused it to stick around for millennia, right up to our present day.

Yet for all of that, what does it actually *mean*?

···&···

The fact that you're reading this book right now demonstrates your openness to learning new things.

I myself love learning (and then sharing) underused words.

Let me introduce you to one:

> **aphorism** | [1]*A pithy observation which contains a general truth*

Stated another way, an aphorism is a way of saying a lot with a little. And as far as aphorisms go, you'd be hard pressed to find a more shining specimen than "Know thyself." After all, it's only two words. Yet despite its compact size, it packs a real punch. Socrates himself was purported by Plato to have held the saying up as the exemplar among aphorisms, "twisted together, like a bowstring, where a slight effort gives great force."

As it happens where "Know thyself" is concerned, I'm not the first to pose the question "But what does it *mean*?" And Socrates would have responded—as he undoubtedly did with countless pupils of his own—that it's not so much important what it means, as what it means *to you*.

In this way, aphorisms are like fine art. Both have genuine value. But the specifics of that value lie in the eye of the beholder. *It's personal.*

I'll never forget my first trip to Paris. I suddenly found myself in the heart of art and culture. Sculptures and paintings I'd seen countless times within the pages of books or depicted in films were suddenly right there before me, mere inches away. And not replicas, mind you. The *originals.*

I remember one Monet hanging at Musée d'Orsay: a golden field dotted with flowers below a blue sky with puffs of white clouds. To describe it to you in words, it was nothing special. Another painting of another landscape. To be honest, I can't even recall the name of the painting; I can only say that its name wasn't a key part of my experience.

I stood so close I could have traced the brushstrokes with my fingertips. I considered the *real person*, long since deceased, who'd been alive and vital, and who had painted this very work onto what was once a blank canvas. I wondered how long it had taken him to complete it, whether he'd ever doubted his talent, and what he'd have thought at the time if he'd known that some of his works would one day be bought for over eighty million dollars apiece.

All the while, it occurred to me that there was nothing preventing someone from destroying this masterpiece in an instant if they'd had a mind to. There was a vulnerability to it somehow. All I know—is that I cried.

My encounter with the Monet could never have been what it was unless I'd created space for unhurried reflection and allowed things to get personal.

Know thyself.

So often anymore, amid the onslaught of words, we just want someone else to *tell* us what things mean. "Don't make me think; I've got 79 unread texts, emails and social media alerts to get to." We've lost patience, and with it the ability to *come* to conclusions rather than *jumping* to them.

I don't suppose much of what Socrates hoped to impart to his students would have sunk in if they'd sat around the steps of the Parthenon all day, checking their Instagamma accounts instead of contemplating what he had to say.

It seems ironic, then, that we'd ever expect someone else to be able to spell out for us the significance of "Know thyself." You must know *yourself* what "Know thyself" means.

That said, I'll share with you some starter thoughts to get you going—a few notions of my own regarding this **tried-and-(still)-true** axiom. As with every bit of wisdom and advice you'll find throughout this book, it'll be up to *you* where you take it from there.

(Still) **TRUE**

The more I inspect this little gem, the more facets I glean from it.

As I touched on above, I certainly hear an admonition to discover or verify things ("know") *for yourself*, rather than taking them at face value or relying on hearsay. We all rail against "because I said so" as teens; and yet, so often as adults, we default to adopting positions and beliefs based on whoever happens to be the loudest, most popular or most influential at the moment. As such, I suspect that the value of independent thinkers will only increase as time goes by.

The ancients believed that to "Know thyself" was to see a glimmer of the Divine, a common thread linking humanity. In this light, to reflect on ("know") *why* we ourselves think and act and react the way we do can provide vital insight into others—what we refer to as *empathy*. We can't hope to deeply understand or connect with others if we are not in tune with ourselves.

Along those lines, the Greeks of Socrates' day acknowledged that "Know thyself" was tantamount to "*Be* thyself." Live wholly and freely, unshackled by the expectations or preferences of others.

Seen from yet another angle, "Know thyself" also carries a sense of minding our own business. If we were to focus on ("know") *our own* flaws and shortcomings, and to continually commit to the hard work involved in personal change, we'd find ourselves with precious little time or energy to worry about what everyone else is doing.

Not TRUE

On the other hand, "Know thyself" hardly means to know *only* thyself. A focus on self and self-interest at the expense of others is *egoism*. And the world has known innumerable atrocities as a result of it.

Nor does "Know thyself" suggest that we can somehow, through enough introspection, achieve ultimate and complete self-awareness. That which ceases to grow—*dies*.

And while "Know thyself" may caution us to be realistic about our own weaknesses, that *does not* imply that we should do so at the expense of being realistic about *our strengths*.

When one of the kids I mentor gets down on themself which they often do, one of my go-to responses is "Tell me three good things about yourself." The first time I ask this, the reaction is usually the same as if I'd asked them to divulge their deepest and darkest of private secrets to me. Awkwardness. Squirming. Grimacing. And inevitably, a drawn-out "Uhh... I don't know." After much cajoling, I may get a sort of backward concession, such as "Well, I guess my vocabulary isn't terrible."

But ask them to tell you about their *failures*, or the things they wish they could change about themselves—well, *now* you've got yourself a conversation.

I'm famous for saying that adults are just kids in older bodies. So it is not surprising that I often encounter reactions similar to those above among friends, conference attendees, readers—just about anywhere really.

Most people are adept at exclaiming their own faults. Sometimes it's even an ongoing conversation in their head. But identifying and speaking about their *positive* qualities feels—wrong somehow. Like conceit. Yes, in certain social settings, people might brag about this ability or that exploit.

But it seems to me that, in real conversation away from the crowds, the majority of people tend to define themselves in terms of their shortcomings and not their strengths.

However, consider this. If we do not identify and feel comfortable with our positive qualities and abilities, how will we be able to develop them and use them to their fullest potential?

By way of example, I know that I am a good teacher. I enjoy teaching. But beyond that, when I speak or teach, *people get it*—often for the first time, despite much prior explanation elsewhere. I see listeners become *learners*. They engage. Perhaps most satisfying is when someone becomes so excited about what they've just heard or read, and the way in which it finally got through to them, that they go and share it with others.

Do I sound like I'm bragging? I hope not. It just happens to be one of "my things." And if I didn't accept this about myself, *I would not be a good teacher*. In fact, I might not teach at all. Knowing that teaching is both a passion and a strength helps me to feel confident when something needs to be learned. And that confidence is actually part of the reason that I am an effective teacher in the first place.

For instance, I can honestly say to a kid who's struggled for years in reading, "Listen, I know you've had a really tough time up to now. But this time will be different. The way I teach is different, so the way you learn will be different. I know you can do this. It's not your brain, it's how you've been taught. It just didn't connect with your style of learning before now. But I understand brains. And if you help me, I can understand how *your* brain works best." Just in saying this with confidence—not false confidence, I really believe it—students approach "this time" differently.

They believe me—because *I believe me.*

I am also a singer. I have a very good ear, and my voice moves easily where I want it to go with little effort. In addition, I'm able to communicate real emotion when I sing. Because   I *know* this about myself, I sing a certain way. I don't hold back. I *believe* that I can tell a story with my voice, and so I *do* wind up telling stories with my voice. If I did not acknowledge that I could sing, I would approach it much differently—perhaps even allowing other perceived weaknesses (such as wishing I had a higher range or more natural grit) to hinder my performance.

If I don't *know* that I have money in my pocket, I cannot spend it. It only makes sense that we can't intentionally use or benefit from something we don't acknowledge that we possess. Likewise, if I don't know the strengths and good qualities I possess, I will not use them very often or very well—if I use them *at all.*

This leaves me dwelling primarily on—you guessed it—my faults. And as I ruminate on those faults, it stands to reason that I will evidence them more frequently. If I'm unable to see my strengths, then I am left to see only my weaknesses. And if I perceive myself as a sum total of my weaknesses, change seems an impossible goal. It is too overwhelming.

All shadow and no light.

In fact, to make changes in an area of weakness implies that the goal is to move toward a position of strength in that area. Yet if I cannot be realistic about my strengths, I have no marker for where I'm headed or how far I've come.

Further, knowing my strengths can actually help me to *address* my weaknesses.

Growing up, it was all too easy for me to fall into unkind conversations with friends while people-watching. I'm embarrassed now to admit it, but we would make sarcastic and hysterical comments about those at the mall, or in an airport, or passing by on the street. Some years back, I realized that this was not a quality that I wanted to keep. It was treating people as "things" for my entertainment, and I didn't want to do that any longer. However, I acknowledged that compassion and listening were among my *strengths*. In identifying these strengths, I was able to apply them to the people that would otherwise be the subjects of my not-so-nice asides. I would think something like, *If I were to sit down with that person, what would he tell me about his life? What is hard for him in life? What does he like to do for fun? When is the last time he got to do that?* This imaginary "listening" brought my compassion to the forefront, and being witty at the person's expense just didn't seem all that appealing anymore.

By using my strengths to redirect my thoughts, I was able to see real change in an area of weakness.

Know thyself.

What are your own strengths? I hope you're up for a challenge. Grab a piece of paper and write down three things that are strengths or positive qualities you possess. Strip them down to this form: "I am _____." This may make you feel uncomfortable, but that's why it's called a *challenge*. And don't ask others, "What do you think are my good qualities?" Take the time to work through identifying them yourself. Go ahead. I'm not kidding. Take a few minutes and do it now.

All done? Now, take that list with you for a week. Put it someplace where you'll see it several times a day. And act on those strengths. If you wrote "I am a good cook," then use your cooking to make something special that will cheer someone up. If you wrote "I am an encouraging person," then remind yourself of that and look for opportunities to encourage those you encounter.

"Know thyself" practiced out of balance results in self-loathing or self-conceit, neither of which is virtuous. You can be realistic about your good qualities and still be humble. I've often suggested that humility does not mean being silent or demure, but rather knowing your rights and then willfully setting them aside for the benefit of someone else. Similarly, holding an accurate perception of your strengths is the only way to put those strengths to use in positively influencing the world around you.

Questions & A Challenge

1. How well would you say you "know thyself" at this point in your life?

2. What's one facet of yourself—habits, traits, motivations, emotions, thought patterns, etc.— that still feels like more of a mystery to you than a known element?

3. This chapter covered a lot of ground. What is one specific concept that caught your attention and that you'd like to spend some more time pondering? Write it down, or if you're in a group, consider sharing it aloud.

CHALLENGE: This first chapter poses its own challenge, but it's worth repeating in hopes that seeing it again here, you'll *stop now and do it*. Write down three things that are strengths or positive qualities you possess. Strip them down to this form: "I am _____." This may make you feel uncomfortable, but that's why it's called a *challenge*. And don't ask others, "What do you think are my good qualities?" Take the time to work through identifying them yourself. When you're finished, take that list with you for a week. Put it someplace where you'll see it several times a day. And act on those strengths.

glass

GROWING UP, we had one TV in the family room. Now every member of a household has at least one, as well as hand-held devices on which to watch programming of choice in separate rooms.

If a movie were rented, it involved discussion. You got to pick the movie tonight, and Timmy got to pick it next time. But then in came DVR, Netflix, multiviewer cable and a host of other options. Sure, no one is in the family room anymore; but it's a small price to pay for getting exactly what we want when we want it.

Even on planes, if a movie were available, it was one movie, shown on one or two large drop-down screens; your option was to plug in the bulky headphones and get the sound—or not. On our 20-or-so-hour flight to China in 1988, that movie was *Moonstruck*, starring Cher (showing on continuous repeat there... and back). Now, most flights have individual screens on chair backs, allowing you to choose from hundreds of shows, movies or music channels. You have only to tap a button or two to instantly tune into precisely what *you* want—and instantly tune *out* the people around you.

Family vacations by car? If the radio was on, it was usually your father's choice or your mother's. As kids, you consequently wound up listening to a lot of music you wouldn't have chosen otherwise; but you were exposed to a lot of music history in the process. On today's road trips, each passenger is safely nestled away under hoods and hats and against pillows, donning headphones connected to personal devices and apps that pump only—and *exactly*—what we want to listen to. Don't like something in your own mix? Just swipe it into oblivion.

Speaking of car trips, we no longer need even tolerate temperatures that do not suit us. No more cracking your window a hair if your wife's feet were cold and she wanted the heat higher. Now, we can just set the temperature for *our half* of the car exactly as we each like it, right down to the degree.

Don't like the opinions or interests of someone online? Hide. Block. Unfriend. Unfollow. And lickety-split—you can restore the soothing equilibrium of a world that looks, talks and acts exactly like *you*, 100% of the time.

I read AI is now able to write entire novel-length books. Soon, users will be able to answer a hundred or so questions about what they want their reading experience to be like, and an algorithm will write an entire book based on those criteria. So if you want a story about a tall, dark and handsome elf named Nomar who has mother issues and goes on a quest to find true love with a mermaid, and which has a classic "happily-ever-after" ending—your wish will be granted. Just **click-click-click** what you want, and you'll be able to enjoy a story you basically wrote for yourself to read.

The upward arc of technological advancement allows an ever more customizable and individualized experience for nearly everything. It's nothing short of miraculous.

Welcome to Planet You.

And, frankly, that terrifies me.

It's like that moment at the end of *The Twilight Zone* episode where the realization hits too late—when the door to the alien spacecraft is closing on the eager earthling passengers just as the lab assistant runs, breathless, onto the scene and shouts from a distance: "Don't get on that ship! The rest of the book, *To Serve Man...* it's... it's a ***COOKBOOK!***"

The more we indulge our own preferences and egocentric urges, the more our ability to compromise or to show compassion is lost.

In other words, when everything is about *me*—empathy dies.

We begin to perceive that *my* music,

my movie choices,

my preferences,

my opinions,

my world view,

my values...

are *the right ones*.

Thus, by default, the choices and perspectives of others are *wrong*, or at best sub-par and deserving of criticism.

And let's face it—technology has made even criticism easier than ever before.

Your dissatisfaction and disapproval need not be anything dire. Don't like someone's outfit or haircut or body shape? Make a quick meme of them and shame them on social media. In minutes, you'll have a throng of "friends" showing their agreement and confirming just how right and smart and clever you are. But you already know this because you are, after all, *you*.

You see, what happens is that the lines between digital customization and *people* customization have begun to erode. People become more like shows or songs or avatars that I either like—or love to hate—depending on how closely they align with my own view of how things should be.

As I'm writing these words—and in what seems an impossibly short time—it's even become commonplace for world leaders at the highest levels to have daily "Twitter battles" replete with name calling, body shaming, racial slurs and more.

And this is the stuff that, like that old *Twilight Zone* episode, gives me a good dose of the willies.

Consider the implications of a world where we the inhabitants no longer possess the character, the skills or the desire to compromise or empathize with the others around us. Imagine the personal and interpersonal ramifications inherent in a society that no longer remembers how to share common experiences, to listen patiently to differing viewpoints, to find solutions for the greater good rather than only what feels good to me in this moment.

And, so what if it's true? Technology is going to move ahead whether we like it or not. Are we simply doomed to some Orwellian fate? Or is there something we can do about it?

One thing I have learned is that worry serves no purpose other than to waste otherwise good moments in the present.

I am also convinced, however, that we *always have a choice*. I cannot choose for a society, or even for a single other person. But I *can* choose what I myself will do, how I will live—right now.

TRIED

People who live in glass houses shouldn't throw stones.

Growing up, we still heard this saying from time to time (though, admittedly, mostly from my grandparents and their friends). At this point in time, however, I don't believe I've heard anyone utter the words aloud in three decades.

That's a shame, because it's a beautiful and succinct analogy that holds timeless instruction on empathy.

In actuality, this **tried-and-(still)-true** tidbit had been in use for a good long while before it ever graced my ears as a child in the '70s. (And I'm hoping by means of this book—and with *your* help—to keep it around a while longer.)

Perhaps you'll recall having read excerpts from *The Canterbury Tales* in high school. Well, for that, you can thank (or curse) a guy by the name of Geoffrey Chaucer. Like him or hate him, he had a way with words. In fact, he is known to this day as the Father of English Literature and was the first poet to receive the honor of being buried in Poets' Corner within Westminster Abbey in London.

Well, around 1385, Chaucer also wrote a piece by the name of *Troilus and Criseyde*. (And if you're one of those people like me who just needs to know these things, it's pronounced "TROY-ill-loose and cris-SAY-duh.").

In this story of love and loss, we find this now-cryptic pair of lines:

> *"And forthi, who that hath an hed of verre,*
> *Frocast of stones war hym in the werre!"*

I know what you're thinking: *Well said, Geoffrey! My thoughts exactly!*

Or not.

As we're traversing the realm of empathy, let's do our best to practice some with 600-year-old Geoffrey. Remember: *when he wrote these words*, people not only understood him perfectly, they thought he was kind of cool. Like Elvis or James Dean. They couldn't get enough of him. And if they'd had the Internet, he would have turned up on one meme in ten.

So the problem with his words isn't him. It's *us*. (Keep an eye out for this theme throughout the remainder of this chapter.)

Anyhow, let me provide a quick glossary for you:

forthi	—	so
who	—	he
hath	—	has
hed	—	head
verre	—	glass (French)
frocast	—	from casting
war	—	beware
hym	—	him
werre	—	war

Popping those into the text, what Chaucer's original audience heard was something like this:

"He who has a head of glass,
from casting of stones he should be beware in war."

It wasn't until another nearly 300 years had passed that another famous Englishman, George Herbert, dusted off Chaucer's words, modified them a bit, and spoke them anew to the audiences of his day:

"Whose house is of glass
must not throw stones at another."

Move forward another hundred years or so, and Benjamin Franklin reprised it this way:

"Don't throw stones at your neighbors,
if your own windows are glass."

The point I hope you're getting so far is that a bunch of pretty smart people have found truth in this saying for a very long time and have done their level best to keep it alive.

And the fact that it has hit home with people from all walks of life for the better part of a millennium is a pretty good indicator that there's still wisdom to be found here *today*—right now, as you are reading.

...&...

Ironically, we live in an age when it's never been more accurate a metaphor to say that we each live in a *glass house*, with computer screens acting as constant windows that peer into a million neighbors' yards.

And we're all quite aware that those neighbors are peering right back. We spend our time taking selfies from 25 angles to choose the one from the bunch that hides the most flaws. Then we brighten our eyes, whiten our teeth, smooth our skin. We add filters that make every shot a mood study. And we're always happy—or at least doing something incredibly interesting. Finally, we plaster our self-made works of art across our walls of glass, creating visions of blissful and perfect lives.

But there is an *awful lot of glass* to cover. So what do we do? We hunker down on a stool in a tiny corner of our glass house, secretly scanning the surrounding yards with high-powered binoculars and telescopes, hoping to catch a glimpse of the lady next door with her curlers on and her make-up off, or of the guy across the way with his beer gut peeking from below his stained T-shirt. And like a P.I. on a stakeout, we snap our spy-cam photos—and plaster those between our own glamor shots to fill the spaces between.

Oh, I know. *You* don't do that. You're quite *nice*.

Read on.

(Still) TRUE

To set the stage, I want to ask you to go beyond mere reading for a bit and to actually take a moment, as best you can, to imagine that a certain personal situation is true and happening to you right now.

Envision it. Feel it. React to it.

I want you to imagine that a concerned friend has emailed you a link to a social media post in which you've been the topic of discussion, but yet in which you have not been tagged. You follow this link and find that a group of people—some of whom you know, but many whom you don't—have posted a less-than-flattering candid picture of you (or perhaps of your kids). You don't know where this picture has come from, only that you didn't take it. The caption added to this picture is ridiculing. What a mess you are. How delusional you are. How monstrously un-cute your kids are. What a god-awful spouse you married, and how it's no wonder that rumors are circulating that you've been cheating with someone else who is named in the post.

Below this is a long list of comments where "friends" and strangers alike are joining in to add their two cents, mostly agreeing, really ramping up the humor of it. Adding more pictures designed to humiliate or embarrass. They jab at your body shape and how you've really let yourself go. One person even goes so far as to say your "very existence is an insult to humanity." Another says they are "surprised evolution allowed such a step backward." You scroll and scroll, but it never seems to end.

How would you react? How would you *feel*? Would you keep reading, driven to know every rotten thing people had to say, to see all of the photos of you at your worst plastered on the glass walls of other people's houses? Would you add a comment to spite them, call them out or express how hurtful this was?

Some years back, I was mentoring a group of guys who were hanging out in my living room on a Monday night. The purpose of the group was essentially to create a safe place where *very* different people who might never consider being friends "on the outside" could come together, talk about real life, and discover that we are more alike than different. They wound up forming a shining example of brotherhood, and they remain pretty close even more than a decade later.

While munching on some pizza before things officially got started, the guys got into a full-blown hate storm on pop music megastar Britney Spears. She was a train wreck. A loser. A psycho. A slut (but they wouldn't mind "getting a piece before it was all used up"). They laughed raucously about the new *South Park* episode in which a caricature Britney is so depressed that she takes a gun and kills herself in front of the show's "kids."

At first, I let the guys go on. I wanted to observe more about how they perceived the world and the people in it. I soon began to see that they didn't think of Britney as a real *person*. She was just a sort of fictionalized character devised solely for the entertainment or the ridicule of the masses.

Britney had recently had the infamous head-shaving incident. She'd not yet lost the baby weight and wasn't the newest kid on the block anymore. And now, due to the odd behavior, she'd lost custody of her children. She'd had two failed marriages, one bitter. Her parents were fighting for control of her finances.

As I listened to this fantastic group of guys rip her

to shreds, I actually welled up. I had to leave the room for a minute. All I could see was a young woman in her mid-twenties, suffering badly from postpartum depression among other things, having just had her children—the most important people in her life—taken away from her, while being smeared across the news and tabloids the whole time.

It soon became publicized that a company had all but finished a documentary about Britney's life and tragic death. It was actually posted that they were "just waiting for her to commit suicide so they could finish it and release it."

Please—stop and consider the *real person* here. Take a few minutes with it.

Imagine it was you.

Imagine it was your sister.

Your daughter.

Why is any of this amusing or entertaining? Try to defend it to yourself.

While scrolling through my social media accounts, I saw friends and strangers alike behaving very similarly regarding Caitlyn Jenner (formerly Bruce). Comments were truly horrific. Judgments were made on every front: moral, ethical, spiritual, parental, personal. Sneering, dogmatic opinions about eternal destination. One comment even asserted that it would have been better if Jenner had been aborted.

Let me say that I'm not faultless here. I've found myself rolling with "creative humor" where other people are concerned. Sometimes, they've been in my physical space (e.g., at the airport or a restaurant). Sometimes, it's a celebrity. But I have to say, whenever this has happened, I wind up feeling pretty awful soon afterward—to the extent that I've become much more aware and much less likely to join in.

How do we justify this behavior in ourselves? No matter how many angles I try to view it from, I only come up with something dark inside of us that leads us to think this is OK.

Here are a few options:

1. "Your glass house is enormous, so if I throw rocks at it, you probably won't even notice; and if you do, getting it fixed is no big deal."

That is, we believe that people are deserving of our ridicule simply because they have a higher degree of notoriety, income, beauty or talent in some area than we have. And that doesn't apply solely to the rich and famous, but to our treatment of anyone we perceive has it better than we do. Our boss. The "golden boy" football star or head cheerleader at school. The neighbors down the street who just bought their third new car in as many years.

2. "No real people live in your glass house, so it's OK to throw rocks at it."

That is, we do not think of such people as people *at all*, but rather existing only as objects for our consumption or entertainment.

3. "All other glass houses only exist to reflect my own glass house."

That is, we think of *most* people as objects on our stage rather than as real people, so those in a higher income bracket are no exception.

4. "Your glass house seems better than mine, so I'll throw rocks at it to make my own glass house seem more desirable."

That is, we stalk and gossip about these people (let's call it what it is) as a result of jealousy at what they've achieved that we have not; it is our way of bringing them down to size so that we can level the field in our own minds.

5. "I am a rock-thrower by nature and I don't plan to stop anytime soon, so I aim at the glass houses of neighbors least likely to call me out on it."

That is, we have ugliness inside of ourselves all the time; and these people are "safe" to unleash it on, because we will never know them. So we can purge the junk inside without interpersonal consequences, rather than letting it out on the people in our everyday circles, which would come at a cost.

As for myself, it's usually that I've somehow forgotten that each person around me is just that—a *real person*, with a *real life* that's just as important and challenging as my own. It feels more like watching life as a movie and making fun of actors, than it does like I'm doing what I'm really doing: being judgmental and unkind.

I hate to say it, but it's also a form of arrogance: *I'm so much more wonderful and stunning and together than that person.*

I recall an instance when I found myself sharing with my grandmother online images of stars whose plastic surgery had been botched, permanently disfiguring their faces. Why did I feel she needed to see that? Or for that matter, that I did? Why do any of us feel it's entertaining when someone who was once valued for their beauty, makes desperate attempts to remain youthful or to stay relevant?

Or when couples divorce and have nasty custody battles that hurt one another and their kids?

Or when they crumble under life's pressures and become drug addicts?

There's no other way to put it. *It's just ugly.*

And I've only touched on those people whose glass houses seem distant to us, never mind the stones we throw at the next-door neighbors.

At our co-workers.

At people in our friend circles.

At our spouses.

At our parents. Our siblings. Our children.

See, I think it's easy for us to think of the rich and famous as living in glass houses. We say to ourselves, *You put yourself into a glass house, making yourself fair game for scrutiny when you pursued a life of fame* (we even refer to it as being "in the public eye").

By allowing ourselves to engage in *any* kind of stone throwing, we are reinforcing a *flaw* in ourselves every time—a rift in our character that makes it easier for the bile to spill out onto the people in our everyday lives.

You can't practice hatred by throwing stones from out of the corners of your glass house and expect it not to crack and fracture the surrounding glass, revealing itself in other areas. Like the windows of a submarine, as pressure increases, even the tiniest fissure spreads, causing exponential (and, sometimes, irreversible) damage.

The truth is that we *all* live in glass houses. We strive to keep those windows plastered with images of our best selves. But just as we peer out from between them to catch glimpses of the neighbors at their lowest, it's not as difficult as we'd like to imagine for those with ill intent to catch *us* at our worst.

So what's the solution to all of this shattering glass?

Empathy.

Empathy finds the threads of similarity and weaves them tighter, rather than picking at the areas of difference until they fray.

Empathy draws on common personal experience. It says, "I will treat you as I want to be treated. I will treat you as I would want my mother, my brother, my daughter to be treated."

I once heard someone say, "No one cares if the organ donor that will save your mother's life votes the way you do."

Put another way, imagine that you are in a hospital waiting room while your son (or daughter or mother or spouse) is undergoing brain surgery. You learn that the two others in the waiting room with you also have a son undergoing the same surgery. Really take a moment to "be there," to imagine and experience as much as possible what you'd be feeling, thinking and valuing most if you were in this circumstance. Between pacing and wringing your hands, you learn through conversation that the other two people waiting with you voted for the other candidate. Or that they are of another faith or sexual orientation or cultural group or economic status.

In fact, let's even move away from the big things to the kind we tend to pick at most often in others, both the famous and the familiar. In that hospital room, suppose that one of the other parents has disheveled hair or gray roots. Extra weight around the middle or flabby arms. Wrinkles or dark circles or messy mascara.

In that seemingly interminable space of time—as each of you waits to hear whether your child will live or die— do you care about *any* of these things?

Would you find yourself hating them? Criticizing? Ridiculing? Hoping to shine a huge spotlight on their perceived flaws or differences? (In truth, would any reasonable person in a similar circumstance *even notice* such things?)

Or would your inclination be to support, encourage, console, and receive whatever they are able to offer of the same in return?

I'm convinced that an acceptance of just how fragile our own glass house really is makes it nearly impossible to reach for those stones.

Not TRUE

Don't misunderstand this all to mean that we should *never* point out bad behavior. Or encourage better performance. Or speak out against injustice. There are times when these things are necessary as part of being a responsible parent, friend, teacher, boss, or citizen in general.

There's an *intent* to throwing a stone at a glass house: *to do damage, to injure.* Ironically, while stone throwing certainly does those things and makes for quite a mess, it rarely results in the other person actually changing anything. Instead, they just get mad at all of the glass you've left them to clean up. And believe me, true to the intent of the original saying, that person is also simultaneously looking for the nearest rock to lob your way at the next opportunity.

The key to successfully delivering a critique to another person is *motive.*

Following are some checkpoints that, if assessed honestly, will virtually assure you'll be heard with minimal breaking of glass.

1. Determine necessity.

Make a habit of answering these three questions when you want to criticize or correct someone:

"Is it necessary for me to say what I'm about to say?"

"What further damage will occur to this person if I don't approach them with this issue?"

"What positive change do I hope for this person as a result of my approaching them?"

If the honest answer to these questions results in little more than "I'm just mad and need to get this off my chest," it's probably best to put off any confrontation. In my own life, I've adopted what I call the "Three-Day Rule." That is, if I feel my own negative emotions roiling, I give myself three days to return to baseline, and then I ask myself those same three questions again (more on this later in the book).

2. Hold yourself accountable first.

It takes wisdom, humility, self-awareness and a good dose of courage to admit that *you yourself* might have contributed to a problem. Going back to our primary analogy of the chapter, this is realizing that my *own* house is made of glass and, therefore, likely has cracks.

Perhaps you are an employer, a teacher or a parent. Might you have been less clear in your communication than you should have been? Might your expectations have been un- reasonable? Might you have subtly incited an incident because your own attitudes toward or feelings about the other person were already negative going into it? Is it possible that you spoke in an unduly harsh way to someone in front of others? Could this situation have an element of "Do as I say and not as I do"?

There have been situations in my own life where, after honest assessment, I really believed that 95% of a problem was due to someone else's bad decisions. But that still left 5% for which I needed to accept responsibility.

In such cases, a sort of relational magic happens if you can set aside your pride and, at least for the initial conver- sation, also set aside what you believe *the other person* has done wrong. Save that for a follow-up conversation. Go to the other person and own your part.

In one case, someone in a position of authority had thrown me under the bus to save herself. This is what owning my 5% looked like for me: "I know we've had some issues lately. In thinking about the problem, I realize that instead of remembering your many positive qualities over the last few months, I've villainized and avoided you. I'm sorry I did that. I know you are a good person."

And what followed this particular acceptance of my own blame was the breaking not of *glass*—but of a wall, a dam. She burst into tears, hugged me, and said, "I know I've been a complete b*tch lately. I'm going to fix the mess I made."

And she made good on that. There wasn't even a need for me to have part two of that conversation.

Let me make clear before we move on that there are absolutely times when a problem arises, needs addressing, and you *are not* in any way at fault. Not every street goes two ways. An employee is coming in late repeatedly. A student just isn't completing homework no matter how much support you offer. A family member or friend has accused you of something you just flat-out didn't do.

The goal of this particular measure of self-assessment isn't to try to find a way to own part of a problem; it's simply to recognize it if it's there.

3. Focus on the person, not the problem.

I devote an entire chapter in my book *The Best Advice So Far* to this topic. But in short, this comes down to being sure we let go of focusing on *what* a person has done (which is usually something that negatively impacts *us*) and commit to discovering *why* the person made this choice. A good practice in empathy would be to pretend the other person is your favorite person in the world (e.g., your best friend, your brother, your mom) and consider what reasons you might come up with for why a *good person that you really like* might have done whatever is in question.

In practical terms, most of us tend to approach correction like this: "You did X, and that caused a problem."

Instead, try a question or invitation, allowing time to really listen, as if to your best friend or your daughter: "Can you help me better understand *why* you did X?"

The answers might surprise you. And often, you'll have helped the person come to *their own* conclusions about what needs to change.

Of course, it never hurts to "throw a bone" first (more on this in *The Best Advice So Far*). In short, where your words can be both honest and relevant, you'll get further with correction if you can lead with one or two areas, past or present, that exemplify what you appreciate about the person or what they have done *right*.

Some people I've known along the way have interpreted this chapter's central quote about glass houses to mean that we should simply move to a brick house *and then* throw stones. They don't disguise the fact that they are stone-throwers; they just tout the philosophy that people should toughen up and stop being so sensitive.

Akin to this take on things is one I encountered in church growing up.

The Christian Bible essentially quotes Jesus as saying, "How dare you talk about the speck in your friend's eye when there is a beam in your own. What a hypocrite! Worry about getting the giant log out of your own eye, and then you'll be free and clear to start pointing out specks in everyone else's eyes."

I can assure you that these verses in no way curbed people's penchant for throwing stones by way of gossip, criticism and self-righteous finger-pointing. You see, when questioned, they simply stated as fact, in hushed and holy tones, that they had indeed, through much prayer, purified themselves—that they'd long ago removed their own beams entirely—and were thus in good standing with the Lord to act as judge and jury concerning others.

To this day, I'm not sure how they missed the obvious hyperbole.

The solution to the problem is neither to barricade ourselves into self-protective or stoic fortresses nor to delude ourselves into thinking that the glass in our own house is somehow special or bulletproof.

Of course, throwing stones isn't just about verbal criticism. It's about our *attitude*. We all know, and too well, that a smile and polite demeanor can hide a world of judgment.

I was talking with a friend recently. I'll call him Ralph here. Ralph's relationship with his brother had been on the outs of late, and he was trying to understand what had happened and what he might be able to do at this point to improve the relationship.

I asked a series of questions. This revealed that the rift had started when Ralph had voiced his stand (e.g., opinions, religious views, moral position and, dare I say, judgment) on his brother's recent decision to get divorced and, soon after, to date someone new. In other words, he'd thrown some stones at his brother's house of glass.

I asked Ralph, "How do you think you'd handle it if you were in the mix with a flamboyant gay guy?"

At first, Ralph looked bewildered. But trusting that I usually have a point to my rabbit trails, he answered. "Well, a few years ago, I actually *was* in the mix with a flamboyant gay man that I needed to interact with at an annual event. And we got along great." It was clear from the phrasing that this was one of very few such people Ralph had ever known, if not the sole example.

I continued, "So, would you say it would feel comfortable for you to use the words 'even though' in describing your relationship with that person? For instance, could you easily complete this sentence, 'I liked the guy *even though...*'?"

Ralph straightened up, answering quickly and confidently. "Yes, absolutely. I feel comfortable saying that I liked him *even though* he was gay, flamboyant and married to a man."

The slump to his shoulders told me that he wasn't expecting what I said next.

"I thought that might be the case, Ralph. *And that's a problem.*"

Stick with me here for what might at first seem off the point.

I love *words*.

There's an inherent power in words. The right word or phrasing used at the right time can earn a first date or seal the impossible business deal. Likewise, a word used carelessly or at the wrong time can start a war.

My curiosity is continually piqued by *connotation*: the *implied* meaning or feelings that become associated with a word or phrase over time among a particular group of people. One example I cite often is *rocking chair*. Here's the dictionary listing:

> **rocking chair** | *a chair mounted on rockers or springs, so as to rock back and forth*

Nothing particularly earth-shattering for a native speaker to learn there.

However, answer the following questions to yourself:

What is a rocking chair made of?

What color is a rocking chair?

Who sits in a rocking chair?

Cultural *connotation* all but guarantees that the majority of people will form an instant *mental image* paired with the following:

> *Rocking chairs are made of wood.*
>
> *Rocking chairs are brown or white.*
>
> *Elderly people (usually "grandmothers") or young mothers sit in rocking chairs.*

If you "saw" something different, it's either because you yourself *had or have* a particular rocking chair that came to your mind—or because you are simply trying to be contrary.

However, there is nothing about the actual definition of *rocking chair* that in any way prohibits it from being plastic, being purple with green polka-dots, or being used by a teenage boy.

Ignoring the connotations of language causes us to falter in our communication (or, worse still, to choose willful deceit).

With this in mind, let's dig a little deeper into that two-word transitional phrase that had my friend Ralph feeling so confused: *"even though."*

Looking up "even though" in a dictionary, here's basically what you'll find:

---

even though | *despite the fact that*

Not very helpful.

Here's where diving a little deeper gets interesting. And please know... I realize that not everyone is a linguistic nerd like I am, so I'll try not to get *too* crazy here.

At the most basic level, "even though" shows *contrast*. In this way, it fits into the family of meanings similar to "but" in logical flow.

Here's the example sentence given by Merriam-Webster:

"She stayed with him ***even though*** he often mistreated her."

We have two facts here:

He often mistreated her.

She stayed with him.

The phrase "even though" is used to join the two facts while adding a logical (or in this case *illogical*) connection.

What would be considered the *parallel* or *expected* or *natural* course of action resulting from "He often mistreated her"? I think most of us would consider it to be something along the lines of "She left him."

By pairing the two facts with "even though," we show a contrast between the actions of the two people—and, in fact, between the people themselves. We're not concerned in this sentence with exploring *why* she acted as she did. But by using "even though," we've essentially created *opposites*:

abuser / victim

mean / nice

As such, while it's not expressly stated in the sentence, "even though" asserts the following strong implication:

S*he **did not** mistreat *him.

In other words, if the speaker of the sentence knew that the woman *had also* mistreated the man, to use "even though" would have been an intentional act of *deceit* aimed at making it *seem that she had not.*

Coming full circle, I'll say it again: "even though" shows *contrast.*

Opposite qualities or expectations.

Yeah, so? you're thinking.

Well, let's revisit Ralph's reply to my probing question:

"Yes, absolutely. I feel comfortable saying that I liked him *even though* he was gay, flamboyant and married to a man."

And here's the diagnostic element. Since using "even though" felt comfortable to Ralph, he had set up a foundational *separation* between himself and the other man. In fact, he'd created logical *opposites*, not merely "differences."

Make sure you grasp this. Read it again if you like. It's key.

When we say (or think, or would feel comfortable saying or thinking)…

"I [nice / positive / right thing] ***even though*** that person _____"

…we've revealed that we believe whatever fills that blank is [***not nice / not positive / not right***].

We are in short saying, "I am good but you are bad."

And that means it's still another stone thrown through your neighbor's glass house.

Now certainly, in some cases, that dichotomy is *true and accurate*:

"Nora loved her brother **even though** he had murdered a man."

It *would* be good and kind and noble of Nora to continue to love her brother. And we *would* consider that her brother was, at least in this regard, *not* good or kind or noble.

But consider this one:

"I love my kids **even though** they are messy."

That's terrific. But make no mistake: a contrast—an opposite comparison—*is* being made here. "I am *not* messy (which, by implication, is the right way to be), so it's mighty big of me to overlook the flaws of my kids." The use of "even though" casts *me* in a favorable light and, therefore, my kids in an ugly one.

The problem comes when we deceive ourselves into thinking that our expression of love or acceptance for someone "even though"... is somehow an indicator that we've become a beacon of true equality.

In fact, it reveals quite the *opposite* about us.

So when someone who identifies as Christian says, "I get along fine with my neighbors, **even though** they are Muslim," it's really saying...

"I am right and good and so big a person that I can get along with those wrong and bad people."

And when my friend Ralph expressed, "I liked him *even though* he was gay, flamboyant and married to a man," he was really saying...

"I—being a straight person of reserved demeanor whose family is doing things the only correct and acceptable way—am by default the moral standard; and yet I'm such a good person that I found it within myself not to mention the flaws and wrongness of that other morally depraved person who really should change to be more like me."

Still not convinced? Then please accept a challenge.

If you don't think this type of comparison is being made when you have an "even-though" view of others—if your claim is that it *does* somehow reflect true equality and that I'm just nitpicking—try flipping your statements around so that *you* are on the other side of "even though":

> "*My kids love me **even though I**...*"

> "*The Muslim family next door gets along with me **even though I**...*"

(And if you're a teen, or you are Muslim, put your parent or Christian neighbor first in those examples.)

When I asked Ralph to swap the order of *his* "even though," here's how he completed it:

> "*My flamboyantly gay associate liked me **even though I**... am a self-righteous and judgmental jerk.*"

Do you see the realization Ralph had about his own glass house here?

The fact is, "even though" statements feel bizarre where a mindset of *true* equality exists. Consider:

"We have been friends since childhood *even though* she has brown hair."

Weird, right? But *why*? Well, the reason such a statement likely feels off to you is that, *in your heart of hearts, you truly don't care about hair color*. You may notice it. You may even appreciate or admire it. But at the core of your being, where truth lies, hair color simply holds no connotations of right or wrong, good or evil. It just *is*.

True equality draws no lines. But neither does it draw attention.

True equality is invisible to itself. It forgets that it even exists.

"Even though" isn't just about the words you happen to say aloud.

It's an attitude, a mindset, a revelation of self.

"Even though" is a worldview.

It's a denial of the glass comprising our own house.

And true equality finds little use for it.

In summary, the goal when considering glass houses isn't to shut up, toughen up or clean up. And it's not merely to pretty up our words without addressing our attitudes as well. The solution, arrived at through empathy and humility, is simply to put down the stones.

Questions & A Challenge

1. Do you consider yourself an empathetic person? If so, is your empathy consistent or selective?

2. How do you respond to the viewpoint that reading, taking part in or spreading celebrity gossip is a vice?

3. Can you identify in yourself any "even-though" attitudes you have toward others? What do you make of the claim that such attitudes are an indication of egotism or self-righteousness?

CHALLENGE: For the next three days, cut out all forms of "stone throwing" you can think of (e.g., reading click-bait opinion articles about celebrities, roasting anyone on social media, gossiping with friends about anyone, etc.). Keep a journal during these three days, writing down every opportunity for "stone throwing" that presents itself, and whether you succeeded or failed with it. At the end of the three days, write down what you notice about how the experiment affected your empathy, relationships and overall state of mind.

𝒮

baby

"**Y**OU *ALWAYS* HAVE A CHOICE.

That is the central theme of my first book, *The Best Advice So Far.* I've spoken or written those words literally thousands of times over the years. And I still feel and see as much power in them today as they've ever held—the power to transform the way we view and live life.

Yet I realized recently that, much of the time, the stories and advice featured in my first book and on my blog (TheBestAdviceSoFar.com/blog) are centered on *macro-level change*:

- You aren't doomed to misery throughout your college years and thereafter for the sake of grinding through a major and career you hate—even if diverting from the original plan conflicts with the perceived expectations others have of you.

- You are not "stuck" in that job. It's within your power to choose to walk away from it and do something else (as impossible as that may seem in a moment).

- You don't need to stay with that **B.E.A.S.T.** (i.e., **B**ig **E**nergy-**A**bsorbing **S**tupid **T**hing) that's sucking the life out of you. (This is such an important topic that, if you haven't yet read *The Best Advice So Far*, please contact me at the email address on the author page of this book, and I'll personally send you that chapter for *free*).

In essence, each of these is a way of saying, "You can *stop doing that—right now*—and make a whole *new* choice."

And that is 100% true. You can. Many times, you *should*.

But it isn't the *only* option. Not by a long shot.

In this chapter, we'll explore another possibility...

Staying.

You see, staying is *also* a choice. Sometimes, it's even the *best* choice—one that involves countless other choices that have the ability to breathe new life into a tired, difficult or even painful situation.

TRIED

Don't throw the baby out with the bathwater.

Young Tommy hails from a stable middle-class home where his parents are fairly well respected in the community. However, like many teens, he's angsty—afret over what to do with the rest of his life. At sixteen, he packs up and runs away to join—you guessed it—*the Franciscan monkhood.*

OK, maybe you didn't guess it after all.

Even less likely would be if you guessed that we were talking about Thomas Murner, born in 1475, just over the border from Germany, in France.

From all accounts, Thomas wasn't the most fun-loving kind of guy. No Friar Tuck, if you will. In fact, he spent a lot of his monk time engaged in the equivalent of social media feuds with other key figures of his day, most notably the famed Protestant thought leader Martin Luther. And in a 1512 missive entitled *Narrenbeschwörung* (if you'd rather not try pronouncing that, stick with *Appeal to Fools*), Murner dishes it hard with the headline "***Das Kind mit dem Bade ausschütten.***"

Oh, no, you *didn't*, Thomas!

Yes. Yes, he did.

But if you're still not sure exactly what it was he *did* do, the direct English interpretation brings us back around to the adage we're currently considering: "Pour the Baby out with the Bath." And it's abundantly clear from the satirical context that, well... only a fool would do such a thing.

As pithy a sound bite as I'm sure it was at the time, Murner's words didn't wind up getting much airtime in non-German-speaking circles. In fact, it wasn't until 350-ish years had passed that another Thomas translated the words into English.

Enter Thomas Carlyle. As it so happened, Carlyle was a bit of a nerd for all things German. And so, in another word-slinging battle on American soil, he translated Murner in his (unfortunately titled) antebellum essay, "Occasional Discourse on the N***** Question":

> [I]t is important for us, in reference to this Negro Question and some others. The Germans say, "You must empty-out the bathing-tub, but not the baby along with it." Fling-out your dirty water with all zeal, and set it careering down the kennels; but try if you can to keep the little child!

I'll come back around to Mr. Carlyle later on. But for now, we know how the saying made its way to a new continent and language. It's not a pretty story. But then again, all this throwing of babies is no pretty image.

...*&*...

My goal with this book is to take these **tried-and-(still)-true** sayings and help a new generation understand, connect with and live by them once again. So rather than leaving this oldie-but-goody as no more than a vague notion, let's bring it close to home with a bit of... let's say "visceral visualization."

I present to you Exhibit B (for "Baby").

When most people hear the word "baby," they envision a wide-eyed little wonder like the one on the Gerber label.

Awww. Babies are adorable. Babies coo and giggle. Babies think everything we do is hilarious. We want to cuddle them and talk gibberish to them and smell their baby-head smell.

Thing is... babies also *poop.*

In fact, sometimes, babies poop *a lot.* It's remarkable, really, how such a tiny body can even...

But, alas, I digress.

Let us imagine that such plentiful pooping has just occurred courtesy of our imaginary baby.

Back in the olden days, they didn't have disposable diapers.

They didn't have Johnson & Johnson.

They didn't have wipes.

They had cloth diapers that needed to be washed

afterward and reused, and not much else. (In fact, I recently learned that my own mother used cloth diapers even on *me*, and I'm not that old… or so I keep telling myself).

And so the quickest way to restore equilibrium when things got… messy… was to plunk the little tyke into the tub straightaway. For the sake of keeping our mental images consistent, let's make it the small old-fashioned wooden variety.

Almost immediately, that water begins to work its cleansing magic on our baby. But the poop hasn't really gone anywhere. It's just been transferred to the water and diffused (mostly). Suffice it to say that when we're done, no one is going to be arguing to keep that water and reuse it. No, the natural response is to *throw it out*.

But, at the end of that bath, the baby is still sitting right there in the middle of the ick.

What to do? What to do?

Oh, bother. It's all such a nuisance. Let's just throw the baby out with the bathwater and be done with it.

Here's the illustration that accompanied Murner's 1512 book:

I should think the problem here is evident.
And that problem... *isn't the baby.*

(Still) **TRUE**

So often, isn't this our first approach to life? Instead of doing the work of separating the good from the bad when things get... er... poopy, we just want to toss the kit and caboodle out the window and wash our hands of the whole darned thing (in another basin, of course).

But in doing so, we potentially risk missing out on the beauty of what exists *right where we are*, for the sake of imagining that pastures are greener anywhere but *here*.

Maybe it's a job—or an entire career path—that feels like an albatross around our neck. There's no joy anymore, no sense of purpose. It's just a perpetual loop of "SSDD" (Same Sh*t Different Day). Again, there is always the choice to make a *new* choice, to leave it all behind and start over. And often, that's exactly the right choice to make.

But what if there's still a baby there in the murk?

Prior to heading out for a speaking engagement in Charleston, South Carolina, I was in the market for a new pair of dress pants. Upon entering the store, I was greeted by a young guy (we'll call him Dan) who started in with the expected "Can I help you find anything?" Realizing that such positions are often based on commission, I assured Dan that I'd come find him once I was ready to check out.

As is typically the case, I couldn't find a pair of pants I liked in my size. (Fine—if you must know, I have short stocky legs, a skinny waist and a big butt.) So I chose the closest match and went looking for the in-house tailor.

As promised, I found Dan to help me out.

I stood in front of the three-panel mirror on the carpeted riser, with the hems of the new pants pooling around borrowed black slip-ons, as the tailor tucked and made his chalk marks. Before I knew it, I was back in my comfy jeans, and the tailor had whisked the trousers off to the workroom with the promise that they'd be finished in ten minutes. But Dan stuck around to complete the purchase, and so I got to talking (I know, shocker, right?).

I asked Dan if this was his first job and if he liked it. He told me he'd previously worked for a fast-food sub place and then as a waiter at a chain restaurant before this job. He told me that he missed the freedom of wearing more casual clothing to work, but that he guessed this job was a step up for him. His face didn't convince me, so I probed a little further.

"But…?"

Dan shifted his feet and smiled half-heartedly. "Well… there can be tension over who gets to work with customers, because of the commission thing. So you never really get to be friends with anyone here. And I realize it's kind of a dead-end job as far as money is concerned."

OK, so quit, right? Find another job you like more. It's not a bad option, and it certainly beats going to work every day and feeling stressed out, discouraged or lacking purpose.

But that's not the option I posed to Dan. Though I'd heard mostly about the bathwater—what he *didn't* like— I also sensed there was a baby hidden in there somewhere.

"Do you mind if I ask a few what-if questions, Dan?"

"No, go ahead," he said. I could tell he was genuinely

interested in the possibilities at this turn in the conversation, curious.

"What if you chose to transfer care of one of your own rightful customers over to another salesperson every so often, and let them have the commissions, if any? Would the loss on the commission tank you? And how do you think your co-workers would respond?"

The look on Dan's face clearly showed that this was an idea he hadn't even considered before now. "Um... I'm not sure how they'd react. They'd probably think I was up to something. But no, the commissions aren't *that* great, especially if it was only once in a while."

"What if you flat out told them, 'Building good relationships is more important to me than the money, and this is my way of trying to help us all enjoy work more'?"

Dan smiled as the gears began to turn.

"And what could you learn here that you don't already know," I continued, "something that might open doors for you down the line?"

Here, Dan paused, looking quizzical. "I don't really know. I mean, there's not much to the job, really."

"Well..." I thrust my chin in the direction the tailor had disappeared. "Do you know how to tailor a pair of pants? What do you think the tailor would say if you asked if you could observe him sometime, or even asked him to teach you how to do it?"

Again, a grin slid across Dan's face. "Hmmm. I guess that *would* be new. And kind of fun, now that you mention it." Then he added, as if I were magical, "How do you *come up with* this stuff?"

I just gave him a mysterious raise of eyebrow and said,

"Practice."

My pants were finished and Dan led me to the counter to check out. He thanked me a couple of times for the conversation and promised that he'd look around for things to learn and ways to get to know the other workers better. And with that, we said our goodbyes.

Maybe, like Dan, your bathwater is a job you've been slogging through each day for too long.

Maybe your bathwater is a once-romantic relationship where each of you has gotten a bit tired and lazy, clouding your feelings toward the person you fell in love with.

Maybe it's a teenage son or daughter who seems a million miles away emotionally, or with whom every word seems to turn into a fight lately. And it just feels easier to give up.

Maybe it's that book you started writing. Or that good cause you used to champion with passion. Or that dream you once chased, that slowly got pushed out by the daily grind.

The first step is to identify *your* baby, to differentiate it from the surrounding muck. Once you can say, "Yes, there *is* a perfectly good baby here," it's not so hard to remember why you love that baby and to begin draining some of that murky bathwater.

Not TRUE

The tail end of the 1990s was a heyday for email scams and hoaxes. Good luck could be gained, or certain calamity avoided, by sending an email to ten friends. Mrs. Jovann Mafra, a dying widow from Africa, would transfer

23.5 million dollars to you if you'd just provide her with your full bank account information (the saintly dear). One could say just about anything, and people would not only believe it but pass it on to others. (After all, if you didn't, Jesus wouldn't love you anymore).

Among those to hit the scene in 1999 was one entitled "Life in the 1500s" wherein all manner of curious information was set forth. Most versions contained this bit:

> Family members took their yearly bath in May, but it was just a big tub that they would fill with hot water. The man of the house would get the privilege of the nice clean water. Then all the other sons and men, then the women and finally the children. Last of all the babies. By then the water was pretty thick. Thus, the saying, "don't throw the baby out with the bath water": it was so dirty you could actually lose someone in it.

OK, work with me here.

Let's say, for the sake of argument, that instead of the water's just being "pretty thick," it was actual *mud*. No— it was mud made with *fresh cow manure*. If you were to reach in, grab a slimy clod of it and drop it, it would not *splash*, it would **plop**.

Alas, into this bucketful of sludge a baby has been placed. The baby, none the wiser, squirms around having a rip-roaring time of it until it is *completely covered* in muck.

Were we honestly to believe that *no one would have noticed* that a living, breathing *person* was still in there?

That someone placed a baby into this slop and then left it unattended so long that they forgot they'd done it at all? And after all of that, they bent over, picked up this portable receptacle, walked some distance with it sloshing about, and then *tossed* it—never having seen, heard or felt that baby sitting right there the whole time?

Well, if you were one of those people who somehow *did* believe this cockamamie story, all I can say is… actually, I don't know what to say to you.

Yet, ironically, this *does* seem to sum up the way we can get sometimes, doesn't it? Something in our life doesn't go exactly as we'd like, and instead of shaking it off and moving on—letting each day start fresh and clean—we *add to* the junk. We heap on complaints and sarcasm and self-pity until it's just one big swill of bitterness where everything stinks and we can't see anything good at all.

The remedy? Learn to recognize negativity for what it is—and nip it in the bud.

Of course, with reference to the same sensational-istic email from 1999, there's another real-world group of people who have quite the opposite problem. They didn't leave the baby in the bathwater. They never *put* the baby in the bathwater in the first place. Heck, they don't even *have* a baby. No babies for miles around. Still, they fretfully rake through the filth *one more time*, keeping buckets of dirty water around *just in case*.

These are the people who never change *anything* for fear that, if they do, something terrible will happen. Or they get the idea that being a responsible person somehow means sticking with yucky things on principle, no matter what.

If, in a moment of honesty, you see yourself in either of these descriptions, let me gently point out that there's a reason our language has the idiomatic phrase "...to the *bitter* end."

To the worriers and bitter-enders, I'll offer one simple suggestion: you can get away with *almost anything* on a "trial basis." In other words, try not looking at potential change as permanent.

Try a new haircut, nothing drastic. Remind yourself: it grows back.

Borrow a few articles of clothing from a trendy friend and see how you feel in them *for just seven days*. If you don't like it, your paint-splotched parachute pants will still be there waiting for you when the week is up.

Feeling stuck in a dead-end job? Even a career change doesn't need to be permanent if you don't want it to be. Mark your calendar—maybe a date six months from today—and decide to try something new until that time. Tell yourself that, on that date, you'll reassess and either make the temporary arrangement more permanent, or try something completely new. It may even be the step that helps you see the baby in the bathwater of the career you left, allowing you to build on the parts you enjoyed while making a clean break from the parts that were bogging you down.

In closing, there's one more not-true situation that's important to keep an eye out for with regard to babies and bathwater. Remember Thomas Carlyle from earlier in the chapter? The man who penned the regrettably titled essay on slavery? At first read, you may have been inclined to think he was quite the advocate of human rights. Not so.

In his use of the baby-and-bathwater analogy, it's true that the bathwater *did* represent the institution of slavery. However, the "little child" he proposed plucking from the water was hardly gallant or altruistic. Here's a snippet from the rest of the essay: "[The] Black gentleman is born to be a servant and is useful in God's creation only as a servant." In reality, Carlyle merely proposed that slavery be replaced with the lifelong servitude of African people, who would be paid a pittance but never be free.

Here, Carlyle set up what the field of logic calls a *false dichotomy*: either blacks are slaves or blacks are servants. The argument he presented did not allow for any other option but these two. And so, given only these options, he could seem as though he were the hero, swooping in to rescue the baby.

Thing is… it was a *false baby*. A makeshift ragdoll tossed into a tub.

It's a tendency of human nature to justify, rationalize and excuse our bad behavior and choices. Like Carlyle, we use lofty language and create speeches in attempts to convince others (and often ourselves) that it's really all OK. We rationalize abuse. Or we cry and say we didn't mean it or that we're really going to change this time. But all the while, no matter what we seem to discard in a moment, we always hold onto part of it as "the good part."

> "I'm not a racist and a bigot. I'm just extra protective of my family, because 'those people' *do* have a higher rate of committing crimes."

"I don't drink too much. Lots of my friends drink way more than I do every night of the week. I only drink two or three max. I don't miss work because of it. And it really helps me through how depressed I've been feeling."

"Yes, he's hit me a few times, but you should have seen how good he was on our vacation. He just gets stressed out from his job."

Sometimes, a selfish decision is just a selfish decision. A bad idea is just a bad idea. A lie is just a lie.

There's no actual upside to fooling ourselves or others into thinking we've got real babies in need of saving. The best thing to do with our dirty ragdolls is to simply chuck them right out the window with the rest of the gunk.

Questions & A Challenge

1. Having read this chapter, are you able to identify any babies you've thrown out (or been tempted to throw out) with the bathwater?

2. Which scenario from the chapter best represents your tendency: to throw babies out with their bathwater (i.e., quitting or moving on from things too quickly), to hold onto dirty bathwater with no baby in it at all (i.e., sticking with things long after

they've stopped bringing any joy or purpose), or to hang onto dirty ragdolls that should be thrown out (i.e., justifying bad situations rather than putting an end to them)?

3. Based on your answer to the previous question, what is one area where you feel change is due? What is the worst you can imagine might happen if you made that change (paint the image in as much detail as you can)? What is the best you can imagine might happen if you made that change (again, paint the image in as much detail as you can)?

CHALLENGE: This is a mini choose-your-own-adventure challenge. Pick one. (Or complete all three if you're feeling inspired.)

A. In the next week, try doing something different at work, either by changing something about how you relate to others, or by identifying and learning something completely new (whether it's related to your specific job title or not). Talk with a friend about how your experiment turns out and how it affects your feelings about your job or workplace.

B. In the next week, do something completely new in a relationship that's important to you. It doesn't have to be expensive, just out of the ordinary for both of you. Plan it as a team. Then talk together afterward about any benefits, insights or challenges the experiment revealed.

C. What is one change you've been considering making for a while? For the next week, make that change "on a trial basis," knowing you can go back to the way things were afterward if it doesn't work out. Mark the end of the trial on a calendar, then assess the trial on that date. Did it give you any insights or confidence to extend the trial, or even to make the change permanent? Or was there anything you discovered during the trial that you'd like to continue, even if only in part?

gift

L ET'S START THIS CHAPTER with an experiment. Take a moment to recall in as much detail as possible the last time you expressed sincere thanks to someone. Got that image in mind? Who was the person? What prompted your appreciation?

OK, now see if you can recall two more instances from, oh, let's say sometime during the last week. What were the circumstances?

If you're like many people—most, perhaps—you found this exercise difficult. It doesn't mean you're a bad person. It does, however, put a finger on a growing problem in modern society.

As our lives become more and more customizable, pandering to our egocentric natures, empathy isn't the only virtue to suffer. If we're not careful, our expectations that everything be tailored to our precise liking can ironically also chip away at a primary building block of happy living: *thankfulness.*

By way of making the point, let's examine just one indicator of this cultural shift: the thank-you card. When is the last time you either sent or received one?

While greeting cards on the whole haven't faded to extinction quite yet, they are largely allocated to specific holidays and occasions anymore. Birthdays. Bar Mitzvahs. Christmas. Thank-you cards are managing to hang in there, making appearances perhaps after a baby shower, wedding or graduation. But aren't there still plenty of reasons in daily life to express thanks and appreciation beyond such major special events?

Not so long ago, thank-you cards were sent to the host or hostess after a dinner party, or an evening of drinks and cards. Often, a conscientious host or hostess would even send cards to all guests who had attended, thanking them for coming and expressing how enjoyable the evening had been. (I'm not entirely certain whether it's the card-sending that's fallen to disuse, or the dinner parties themselves; but I highly endorse the revival of both.)

Thank-you cards were by no means limited to formal visits, mind you. A neighbor's sharing of her fresh eggs. The lending of a book. A timely ride to the store. Any kindness, great or small, was considered grounds for taking time to express one's thanks.

This being the case, it was quite common for people to have an assortment of thank-you cards on hand at all times, and they were therefore in as frequent a need of replacement as laundry detergent or hair products.

"Well, sure," you contest, "but they only wound up handwriting lots of notes because they didn't have all the means of digital communication we have today."

However, writing a thank-you card isn't just about the *mode*. It's an act of intention that requires *stopping* whatever you're doing and devoting time to thoughtful consideration regarding how you might show your gratitude. And when I asked my opening questions, challenging you to recall the three most recent times you expressed your own thanks to someone, I didn't rule out texts or emails. You see my point; I really don't believe it's that we've merely shifted from one method to another. Rather, it does seem that we've simply become less thankful on the whole.

And yet, to this point, we've discussed only *one* form of thanks, and only in response to those acts of kindness which fully meet our approval: invitations to dinner, the lending of desired items and the like. This is to say nothing of those undeserved extras done for us on a continual basis, and yet which weren't quite what we'd hoped for.

Or the ones we so take for granted that we don't acknowledge them at all.

TRIED

Never look a gift horse in the mouth.

This is certainly a curious admonition, particularly if you've never heard it before.

At first inspection, it may seem like some sort of strange superstition believed to bring bad luck raining down on your head, like walking under a ladder or stepping on sidewalk cracks.

And while there's something about it that hearkens to eighteenth-century Americana, or perhaps even colonial times, this saying—like so many introduced thus far—is a good deal older than even I had realized. No one can say for sure exactly *how* old it is; but while it first appeared in English in 1546, the first record of it was penned in Latin by Saint Jerome sometime around the end of the fourth century A.D.:

Noli equi dentes inspicere donati.

Even if you've never studied Latin, it shouldn't be too difficult to dissect this one:

Noli	—	no / do not
equi	—	equine (horse)
dentes	—	dental/dentist (teeth)
inspicere	—	inspect
donati	—	donated (given)

Again I propose that if a life lesson has managed to hang around since ancient times, it's most likely worth a closer look.

...&...

If you were in the aforementioned superstitious lot, fear not. You're safe.

In actuality, the practice of looking any type of horse in the mouth was more like checking the book value on a used car before plunking down the cash for it.

For example, let's say you happen to be in the market for a new workhorse when, as fate would have it, you come upon a sturdy-looking Clydesdale tethered to a post out front of a farm, along with a big sign:

FOR SALE
GREAT CONDITION
LOW MILEAGE

You wander over to check things out. The horse looks OK as far as you can see. Farmer Joe ambles up, a good-natured old codger, and assures you that Molly here is just about the most reliable and even-tempered creature on God's green earth; and what with her being just seven years old, you're bound to get another good 10 or 15 years of plowing out of her.

The asking price is a bit steep, but you do the mental math and decide that, broken down per year, even at the conservative end, it's a sound purchase. So you seal the deal and off you go with Molly.

Only thing is, two years in, while tilling the field, Molly *ack-ack-acks* a couple of times and keels over, dead as a doornail.

You make the long trek back to Farmer Joe's place, but everything's been boarded up. A dilapidated wooden sign now hangs cockeyed on the very post where you bought Molly. You can just make out the letters in faded paint:

GONE FISHIN'
FOREVER
(TAHITI)

Just then, apparently having seen you standing there all agape and flustered, the neighboring farmer from across the way moseys over and asks if you need help. You explain that you bought seven-year-old Molly from Farmer Joe a mere two years ago and she just croaked.

"Molly?" says the neighbor, scratching his head. "You're sure it was *Molly*?"

"Yes," you assure him, "Molly."

"Well, she weren't no spring chicken," the man explains, still looking puzzled. "I reckon she had to be nigh on…

oh… prolly twenty when you git her. I helped deliver that one m'self."

Twenty?! You fume silently. *Why that good-for-nothing…*

Yes, Farmer Joe is a big fat liar. But you *also* should have known better than to take him at his word. If you'd been a farmer worth your salt, you'd have known to check Molly's teeth before buying her, or at least to have brought along an expert who knew what to look for.

You see, as horses age, their teeth noticeably change. They protrude and push forward with time. And so the teeth of a seven-year-old horse would look quite different from those of a horse of twenty. (Incidentally, this also accounts for another idiomatic expression that's gone out of fashion: "long in the tooth," meaning *old*.)

Of course, nowadays, we've got paper trails as proof. But in bygone times, you had to work with what you had, which generally wound up being the condition of hooves and teeth. And every smart buyer knew to check both of these before shelling out their hard-earned money solely on someone's word.

However…

If Farmer Joe were to have presented Molly to you as a *gift*, why then, for you to crook your finger into Molly's mouth and yank her lips around to check her teeth would have gone beyond shrewd to just plain *rude*.

(Still) TRUE

This seems a good time to plainly state the meaning of our featured **tried-and-(still)-true** saying: *If someone* *gives you a gift, don't inspect it, criticize it or measure it against what you wish it had been; instead, simply accept it graciously and with appreciation.*

Given the fact that this chapter's cautionary advice is at least sixteen centuries old, it's clear that lapses in thankfulness and basic good manners are not a modern phenomenon, but are just part of human nature. Yet I maintain that the more technology and consumer branding seek to tailor to our every whim and fancy, the more entitled we become and the harder it gets for us to accept those things in life which do *not* perfectly suit us—including gifts.

For many, Grandma's gift of the ugly sweater comes instantly to mind. Well, in my case, it wasn't sweaters.

Growing up, my Nana and Grampa on my mother's side were as reliable as Old Faithful. Every year, like clockwork, you'd get a birthday card with a crisp ten-dollar bill tucked inside. As kids, I assure you that we had no complaints. To this day, understanding more fully just how meager of means they were, I still don't know how they managed to do this for each of us in the first round of grandkids.

However, when it came to my father's mother, it was impossible to predict what might wind up bestowed upon you. Here are just a few of the surprises I received from her at tender ages:

A trial-sized tube of toothpaste.

A plastic shoehorn.

A brontosaurus-shaped lint brush.

As a young teen, I received perhaps the most perplexing of her gifts: an empty box. At first, I thought there must have been some mistake, that she'd somehow forgotten to put the actual present inside before wrapping it. But, nope—she meant to give me just that empty box. It was made of flimsy cardboard, some sort of file "drawer," with an inner part that was slightly smaller and slid out of the main unit. In response to what I imagine was a look of utter confusion as I held up my gift, peering inside and shaking it upside down a couple of times, my grandmother proceeded to extol to me at length the virtues and multitudinous uses for what has henceforth been known as *The Box*:

"Look, you can pull this out and push here, and it folds for easy storage when you aren't using it," she explained. "And it fits manila file folders. I kept the ones that came with it because I need them, but you can just get more. Or you could use it as a phone holder, like a little table. Or you could color on it and put rocks in it and use it as a door stopper. Or you could put your secret letters and notes in it…"

I'm not going to lie. At about the 15-minute point of her monologue, I started to sweat a little, eyeing the exits like a cornered bunny looking for a hole in the hedge. If memory serves me right, it turned out to be the momentary distraction of the nearby spiral-corded wall phone's shrill ringing that saved me.

How was a boy of 14 expected to avoid looking into the mouth of such a gift horse? Hold that thought…

There was a commercial spot I came across online for a well-known logo design mill. In the video, a sweet little girl of about seven with shy and hopeful eyes gingerly holds up a picture of a flamingo she's drawn, presenting it to an adult male whose face remains off camera. A brusque and sarcastic female voice-over says, "Need a crappy drawing of a pink bird thing? Ask your niece," at which point the man's hands reach down, rip the drawing from the girl's hands and crumple it into a ball.

Um… wow. And *yuck*.

In truth, despite other changes in society, *most* of us by far still naturally celebrate and display items that children make and give to us. Regardless of their imperfections, artistic value or whether the content depicts our own favorite themes or colors, we *ooh* and *aah* and proudly display kids' drawings on refrigerators, their rudimentary clay handprints on holiday trees.

So… *what*? Are we lying to children, telling them that their gifts are amazing when we know, based on any objective standard, that what they've offered is subpar at best?

No, I don't think that's it at all.

I'm known in my circles for saying, "Adults are just children in older bodies." In that light, consider that those children whose "pink bird things" we rave about and give kisses for… grow up to become the *very same* adults who give those sweaters and shoehorns and empty boxes. As such, I wonder if we could more often access the place inside ourselves that seems to inherently understand with children that *the value of a gift is in the person and not the thing*.

"You spent time and thought on me. *I appreciate you.*"

Incidentally, I used that trial-sized toothpaste my grand-mother gave me. Once I found out what a shoehorn was, I used that as well (in fact, as I've gotten older, I always seem to want one and never have it). I don't think I ever used the lint brush for its intended purpose, but the bronto-saurus *was* kind of cool as it sat on the corner of the little desk in my room.

And if you were to go into my hall closet *right now*, you would find *The Box*—still holding up after more than three decades, and chock-full of "secret letters and notes" from all those years ago.

Nonetheless, if all of this were solely about those times when family or friends offer gifts we might not have chosen for ourselves, I'm not sure I'd have devoted an entire chapter in this book to the idea. In reality, gift horses abound.

Just by way of example, I enjoy language learning using some free apps. Yet I can't tell you how many times I've heard people complain about the interspersed ads (all of which disappear immediately with a simple click each time), the system of gaining or losing points, etc. Truth be told, even I myself have been guilty of complaining aloud to others about translation errors, lack of ability to contact the app creators, or the seeming inanity of some of the exercise sentences.

Then I remember: *it's free.*

How many times do we wind up grumbling that a free coupon has an expiration date that's too tight, a free sample handed out at the grocer or department store is too small, or a discount on an item we'd like to purchase is too stingy?

But let's not stop there. Thankfulness is a *mindset* that notices and appreciates *all of the many free gifts* that come our way daily.

Sunshine is a free gift. As is rain (just ask anyone in drought-stricken areas of the world). Yet how often do we gripe about how hot (or cold, or wet) it is at the moment?

Hate your job? In addition to making the *choice* to be there, not everyone who wants a job is able to find one. Neither is it guaranteed that anyone have the physical or mental facility to work.

Little Alejandra lives in the "cardboard village" of Coahuila, Mexico. She has one torn rag of a dress and half a pink barrette to her name. She owns no shoes, and her yard is a choking dust lot. Meet her and talk for a few minutes. You'll be hard pressed to come away disappointed with the meal that's next set before you, or the state of your lawn, or the healthcare you have, or the same old clothes in your closet.

Nature, health, conveniences, relationships: none of these are owed to us. Each is a gift. Yet, if we're honest, how many do we wind up "looking in the mouth"? Or simply becoming so expectant of that we overlook them altogether?

Frankly, it's difficult to combat this attitude of entitlement. One thing is for sure: it won't happen by accident.

If you're able, do some relief work in poorer areas of the world. Or perhaps "adopt" a child in need, whom you support monthly and whose picture you keep in plain sight.

Set aside five minutes at the end of each day to reflect on some things from the past 24 hours for which you can be grateful. Perhaps keep a journal or share a few with a like-minded friend.

And don't be afraid to bring back those thank-you cards.

Not TRUE

Working backward a few points, this is not all to say that the right thing to do when grandma comes over is to don those full-body reindeer pajamas she gave you last Christmas and plaster a smile on your face. Likewise, dinosaur lint brushes and fuzzy toilet seat covers need not be kept on hand for fear of causing offense. In those cases where I know I won't really use an item, I tend to appreciate first and then be truthful about intention: "Thank you so much. It looks so warm and you definitely picked a nice color. It *is* a lot bigger than I would wear, though." If the giver kept the receipt and offers it, I may exchange and then send them a picture of me wearing the new item "they got me." If not, I will likely pass the item along to one of the kids I mentor or to a clothing drive, and let the gift giver know how much their thoughtfulness helped someone in need.

Not looking a gift horse in the mouth also doesn't mean never speaking up about bad service, poor work performance, faulty products and the like. In many cases, products and services are not, in and of themselves, gifts; they are purchased and come with certain consumer expectations.

Again, however, keep in mind that the worst we "endure" is better by far than many people the world over could ever dream possible. The perpetual "gift" even in those things we pay for is that we are in a place and time and station in life where we have continual access to luxuries like restaurant meals, tech gadgets, amenities, vacations and such; and that we can afford them.

And bear in mind that most consumer-facing people didn't *cause* the problem themselves. The server didn't overcook your steak. The telephone representative didn't make the faulty smartphone or install the cable TV incorrectly. It's easy to forget this and to wind up speaking to customer service representatives in a gruff, impatient or unkind manner. I usually start interactions by asking their name, giving mine, stating that I know they didn't cause the problem I'm about to report, and acknowledging that I believe it's their aim to help me solve the issue. This absolutely sets the course for the rest of the conversation.

Furthermore, thankfulness isn't just about refraining from complaints. It's about finding the good in things. Like most new skills, it's challenging at first; but as is also the case with most things, it gets easier with practice.

In any area where you find yourself prone to be peevish, try implementing a countermeasure. Not to beat a dead gift horse, but sending regular thank-you cards does wonders in quelling the querulous. Where consumer dealings are concerned, I make it my goal to "reverse complain" far more often than I ever report problems: to call over a worker or manager and tell them what they are doing *right* and *well*, rather than only voicing my thoughts when something goes awry.

Finally—and this is important—not all free gifts are truly free and given with good intention. It's not looking a gift horse in the mouth, for instance, to realize that someone is attempting to buy our silence or forgiveness or acceptance of their bad behavior. Such is the stuff of bribes, manipulation, co-dependence. Even abuse. Moreover, I myself have been witness to gifts resulting from a sense of guilt, laziness, obligation or a combination of the above, with no thoughtfulness behind them whatsoever. While it's important for us to err on the side of gratitude, it's equally essential that we not make excuses for poor behavior, however nicely wrapped. The truth is that such gifts are never freely given; they always come at a cost. If after honest assessment you're inclined to believe that this sort of gift giving is in play, rather than thinking in terms of looking a gift horse in the mouth, a wiser course of action lies in another horse-related axiom hailing from the Trojan War: *"Beware Greeks bearing gifts."*

Questions & A Challenge

1. How often do you think to yourself some version of "I'm feeling thankful right now for _____"? How often do you express this? How often do you express it in ways that go beyond the spoken words "Thank you" or "Thanks"?

2. Are there any gift horses you know you tend to look in the mouth? What insights do you have about this tendency after having read this chapter?

3. This chapter asserts "… it's difficult to combat [an] attitude of entitlement. One thing is for sure: it won't happen by accident." Do you agree? What is one specific and realistic change you might make in your own life that would promote a more consistent mindset of thankfulness?

CHALLENGE: Purchase a pack of thank-you cards that contains perhaps 5 or 10 cards. Hand-write thank-you notes to as many different people as there are cards. Be specific regarding what you are thankful for. Then mail or hand-deliver the cards. Be aware of your own process of writing these notes. Was it hard to think of people to write to? Did it get any easier as you went? Harder? How did you feel when you were finished?

5

penny

IT'S AMAZING how often I find lucky pennies. I'm certain this is partly because I am magical. But I'm sure it is also due to the fact that I am always on the lookout for them. And while this has its own inherent life lessons, I'll leave those deductions to you for the sake of getting to the point at hand.

My luck is not limited to pennies (though other denominations do not carry with them the luck of a lucky penny). Once, as I got out of my car at a convenience store, I found $1.74 in various coinage, strewn across the lot like littered cigarette ashes.

I've found as much as $300 at a time. And there are incredible stories involved, as you might guess. But here, I'd like to focus on a single dollar bill that stands out among my finds. It was night time. I had just made a purchase at a convenience store and tucked the change into my pocket with the other twenty that was in there. On my way out the door to my car, I looked down to my left and there it was, with the orange glow of a street lamp shining down on it like a spotlight on a stage: *a dollar bill.*

Now, I know I shouldn't get as excited as I do. After all, it was only a dollar. And it doesn't even come with the good luck of a penny. But I *do* get excited. I *did.* I marched right over to that dollar bill like a kid on holiday, bent down and scooped it right up into my hot little hand, tucking it into my pocket.

Once home, I reached into my pocket and pulled out the disheveled wad of money, plunking it down on the low table by my front door. I smiled again as I saw the additional earnings, sitting atop the other bills.

The next morning, as I prepared to leave for an early haircut, I began to collect the money from off the table where I'd left it.

Now, a crumple of bills is all well and good at the end of a day; but it *must* be straightened and aligned into a neat stack in order of value (largest toward the bottom) to *start* a day. So I turned and flattened the twenty in my palm. Then the five. Three ones. And lastly—the dirty dollar bill I'd found.

I opened the folded bill to flatten it—and found the flip side of it completely smeared with dog doo. A long, wet streak starting at one side and ending in a sizable mass at the other.   I am not kidding you. I wish I were.

I faced a choice. The easiest—and perhaps most reasonable—choice was to simply adopt an "easy-come-easy-go" attitude and toss that puppy right into the trash. In that moment, still holding the offending object in disbelief, I had to wonder how it had happened. Had someone, at a loss for other means, actually used *money* to remove the unwanted substance from their shoe? Or had there been a car full of chuckling teens parked somewhere nearby the previous night, watching their planted prank for an hour before the final perverse pay-off of seeing a schmuck like me pick it up?

But do you know what I did instead? I took that soiled and stinking bill over to the kitchen sink, cranked on some hot water, and used paper towels and dish soap to clean that dollar. I mean I cleaned it up good: scrubbing, sniffing, scraping, sniffing again. Once the bill no longer registered to my nostrils, I propped it up against some books to dry. I was keeping that dollar, come hell or high water.

Well, this is all very amusing, I'm sure. But I actually *do* have a point.

When I'd found it, the perceived value of that bill was exactly one dollar. The following morning, I'd found that it was marred. Spoiled to some degree. It smelled awful. If I'd thrown it in the garbage, what would its value have been to me? Exactly zero dollars. But, after investing the time and care to clean off George's face and good name, what was the value of that bill to me? *Exactly one dollar—* all the value it had had the night before when I'd first smiled at my good fortune in finding it.

My mother was so proud of me. (I'll introduce her in a moment.)

I distinctly remember the first time I read "The Gift of the Magi" by O. Henry. I was perhaps 11 or 12 and already a hardcore aficionado of vocabulary, and so I found the original 1905 text of the short story to be a veritable treasure trove. I was already thumbing through my trusty dog-eared dictionary before I'd finished the opening paragraph:

> *One dollar and eighty-seven cents. That was all. And sixty cents of it was in pennies. Pennies saved one and two at a time by bulldozing the grocer and the vegetable man and the butcher until one's cheeks burned with the silent imputation of parsimony that such close dealing implied.*

*Three times Della counted it. One dollar
and eighty-seven cents. And the next day
would be Christmas.*

As odd as it may seem, I was already plenty familiar
with the word "impute" even by that young age, having
grown up in a "King-James-Version-only" Baptist bubble.

That left me to explore "parsimony." While I was fairly
certain of the general meaning based on the context, I had
to be sure. After all, words for me have always been about
connotation, etymology, fine shades of difference. If you're
going to use it, really *know* it first.

And as it so happens, I still have that well-loved
dictionary from my youth (for which I paid $4.99) sitting
on my living room bookshelf. Here's what it says (in print
so tiny I can't believe I ever had eyes good enough to read
it):

---

par·si·mo·ny (pär′sə-mō′nē)
n. Extreme or excessive frugality; stinginess.
[<Lat. *parcere*, to spare]
—**par′·si·mo′·ni-ous** *adj.*
—**par′·si·mo′·ni-ous-ly** *adv.*

Ah, I see, I thought, now understanding fully, *so Della
was basically my mom.*

My mother was a nurse and worked hard. Much of the
time we were growing up, she worked night shifts full time
in addition to taking on part-time days. And somehow,
despite this, the laundry was always done, dinner was
always prepared, and the house remained spotless down to
the baseboards.

However, there was a span of years, when my three siblings and I were very young, that my mother did not work, in order to be home with us. During that stretch, her "allowance"—to cover food, clothes, cleaning supplies, medical expenses, pet expenses, gas and anything else— was $126 a week. For a family of six. Hence, she learned to master "the silent imputation of parsimony" with grace.

Powdered milk was mixed with a bit of whole milk to fool us.

Rice might have been served with dinner. Or with milk as breakfast. Adding butter, sugar and cinnamon transformed it into a dessert or snack.

My mother only shopped on Tuesdays, which were "Double Coupon Day" at the local grocery store. We never got to ride in the shopping carriage, because the child seat was taken up with the shoebox packed full of coupons, partitioned with slips of paper that delineated the categories: **PRODUCE**, **BREAD/CEREAL**, **CANNED GOODS**, and so forth.

But coupons alone were for amateurs. My mother was a parsimony *pro*. You see, Fernandes Supermarket also had a rule that if any item were marked differently than it rang up at the register, you got it *free*. And so my mother would pull from the shelves literally every can or box or bag of the item she was after, checking each for the "golden ticket" of the oddball label. Mispriced milk, as I recall, was the Holy Grail.

When she got to check-out, she'd hand over her carefully arranged stack of coupons. If the cashier moved things along too quickly, she'd politely ask them to slow down so that she could compare every item with the pricing monitor. Her eyes would flicker keenly back and forth between the screen and the conveyer, ready to pounce. I'd swear that I could feel the vigilance coming off of her in invisible waves. And when the first wrongly priced item was scanned through, my mom's hand would fly forward in the universal "stop" sign faster than the *blip* could sound. "That one is mismarked," she'd announce firmly. Most often, the cashier would simply cancel the price and move the can of green beans along. But every so often, one would try to get away with a smile and re-ringing at the correct price. My mother's cheeks, like Della's in the story, would flush; but she was relentless. She'd thrust her hand out again. "Your policy says that I get that one free," she'd say with her jaw set and a dare in her eyes.

And this might be the case for a dozen items, depending on the day.

Of course, coupons and erroneous labels weren't the extent of it. If my mother could find a dented can of corn or a torn box of instant potatoes, she'd take it, then haggle with the cashier—and at times a manager—for five or ten cents off based on the imperfect condition.

Expiration dates were more of a suggestion than a rule. In fact, I distinctly remember one particular meal when I asked my mother why the boxed au gratin potatoes had rice in it. And why the rice had legs. Meal worms. And my father had already eaten half his serving.

Thrift wasn't reserved solely for the grocer. Yard sales were clothing stores. And hand-me-downs from female cousins were passed as-is to my sister or, where possible, altered to work for my brothers and me. My mother viewed even roadways as potential shopping sprees. Once, on the way to the beach, my mother edged her way over through heavy traffic and stopped to snatch up a towel that lay abandoned and forlorn in the breakdown lane. Her best friend at the time was mortified, her face aghast from the passenger seat: "I can't *believe* you're pulling over to pick up someone else's *junk*! God only knows where that thing's been!" This did not deter my mother in the slightest. She picked it up gingerly by two corners, holding the crinkled thing out before her for inspection. "See… perfectly usable," she retorted, satisfied. "That'll wash right up and be good as new."

And she *did* wash it up. That towel was used steadily in our house for at least a decade thereafter.

Yet despite the fastidious scrimping, there always seemed to be a mountain of gifts under the Christmas tree and stockings full to the brim. It was only when I was much older that I realized not everyone wrapped batteries separately, or that the individually wrapped pairs of socks or underwear had originally come in a six-pack. A deck of playing cards made for a perfectly peachy present, as did a ball and jacks or a plastic yo-yo. And then there was the perennial favorite of the cardboard-backed game called "Wooly Willy" (who, according to the packaging, had a "magnetic personality") where you would use a little plastic wand to pull metal dust up onto Willy's face to give him hair, a beard, a mustache or eyebrows. All we kids knew is that we got *a lot*, that it was all really cool—and that we felt as rich as royalty.

O. Henry's heroine traded her hair for a watch chain. My mother traded her pride for a shrewdness and frugality that allowed her to raise four healthy kids who lacked for nothing. And as far as I'm concerned, *both* were gifts to make wise men stop and ponder.

TRIED

A penny saved is a penny earned.

It's popularly thought that Benjamin Franklin coined this proverb. He didn't. But get ready for a wild historical tale that, before it's done, will explain why Ben most often gets the credit.

The truth is that the spirit of this adage predates English. However, the first time it appeared in a form clearly recognizable as a predecessor to the modern take was in 1633, when poet-turned-clergyman George Herbert included it in a collection of wisdom. Here's how Herbert penned it:

A penny spar'd is twice got.

If you think back to my opening story about finding that befouled dollar bill, I "got" it once when I picked it up. But then I faced a choice—to throw it away or to keep it. Had I tossed it, it would have been "once got" and "once lost," for a net sum of *zero* "gots." But in finding it *and then sparing it*, it was, in essence "twice got."

If you're still not convinced (or are simply confused), fear not. A little further on, I'll introduce you to another explanation provided by good old Ben Franklin, one you're sure to grasp.

Before we get there, however, I believe George Herbert

deserves a little more time in the spotlight.

As I've already briefly mentioned, George started out as a poet and orator. He was born into wealth, went to an esteemed college in England and worked in academia. His skill as an orator was even called upon by King James I. But for all the posh life offered, George really had a heart for helping the poor and underprivileged. With this goal in mind, he left "the sweet life" behind in his mid-thirties, became ordained by the Church of England, and asked to be the priest of a middle-of-nowhere cow town.

Once there, he realized that his hardworking parishioners were so uneducated—and, frankly, uninterested in liturgy—that trying to teach life lessons from the Bible alone wasn't cutting it. And with the Church far away and certainly not keeping tabs on such a remote parish, he figured he could get away with some unorthodox methods. So he began to build his sermons around very simple and practical proverbs curated from near and far, most drawn from everyday life. By the time he was done, he'd managed to compile a collection containing more than 1,000 tidbits of wisdom. I've introduced you to "A penny spar'd is twice got." Here are just a few more to ponder:

I gave the mouse a hole, and she is become my heire.

All truths are not to be told.

Better a bare foote than none.

Research this entire text as I did, and you'll hardly be able to keep yourself from reading perpetually "one more." They certainly are further proof that principles based in wisdom, however tried, do remain *true*.

Keep in mind that George's parishioners were common folk. I can just imagine George standing stone-faced in his vestments before the congregation—all of whom were likely thinking about the chores and farm work that they'd be better off tending to, but which they'd begrudgingly set aside in deference to this young priest who'd shown them kindness. George stands silently for a few moments before the small, bored crowd. He listens to uncomfortable coughs and scuffing feet—the only sounds in the little meetinghouse as restless men, women and children settle in for the next hour, their mended clothing even now marred with soil or flour. Then he begins the service.

He reads a brief verse from the Book of Proverbs. Then he closes the Bible, leaving it on the lectern and stepping out toward the first row of benches. "Today," he continues, "I'd like to share with you… an outlandish proverb. You won't find it in the Good Book. For while there is certainly much wisdom to be found in its pages, there is *also* much wisdom to be found in the kitchen. In the barn. In the fox's lair and in the bird's nest. Wisdom is all around us, if we will keep an eye open for it."

If this approach weren't enough to inspire, one had to consider George's title for this collective work—which was, as it happens, *Outlandish Proverbs*. Simply put, this title is *brilliant*. One might wonder, "What about a collection of sensible sayings qualifies it as '*outlandish*'?" And that's certainly part of the beauty of the title—that it invokes *curiosity*, just as I imagine it did for those first to hear it 400 years ago. I can just see men who'd been slouching sitting taller. Women cocking their heads.

Children leaning forward.

But the word "outlandish" is the real showstopper, since it is at the very least a *triple* pun.

At the time, "outlandish" would certainly have meant "odd, unfamiliar" even "bizarre," just as it does today. And for that unlearned, untraveled congregation, not only would the vast majority of these "new proverbs" have been unfamiliar, the notion that a priest of the Church of England was supplementing scripture with them would no doubt have seemed bizarre.

But additionally, the word "outlandish" would have been understood at the time to mean "foreign, from afar"— just as George would have been sharing that "Today's outlandish proverb comes to us from India"… or Germany or Sweden. As a matter of fact, nearly three-quarters of the *Outlandish Proverbs* were borrowed from countries other than England.

If that weren't enough, "outlandish" *also* meant "of or related to the outlands; rural." And so, in naming his collection *Outlandish Proverbs*, George was further connecting with his particular audience. In essence, he was saying, "These proverbs are for *you*, the hardworking people of the outlands."

Much respect to you on all counts, George.

George Herbert appears to have completed his *Outlandish Proverbs* just before his untimely death at the age of 39. (Or, perhaps, his passing merely added the final period to what might otherwise have been a much longer collection).

It would be nearly three decades before this proverb would be put to pen again, this time by another English clergyman, Thomas Fuller. In uncanny fashion, his best-known work, entitled (*The History of*) *The Worthies of England*, was also completed—or likewise merely cut short—in the year of Fuller's death, 1661, leaving the saying closer to the wording we know today:

> Now by the same proportion that **a penny saved is a penny gained**, the preserver of books is a Mate for the Compiler of them.

Yet another three decades passed before, in 1694, playwright Edward Ravenscroft again altered the saying in his "Canterbury Guests":

A penny sav'd, is a penny got.

I mention Ravenscroft (whose play under present discussion was, incidentally, a flop) because his use of "got" instead of "gained" was actually a more important shift than one might at first think. That is, "gain"—both then and now—merely meant to acquire or add, while "got" more specifically meant and means "earned" (e.g., "I got $500 for doing the paint job.").

Jump forward 180 years—and hop a pond while you're at it—to the American Civil War.

A few of you may be thinking, "Wait a minute. You said Benjamin Franklin was involved in all of this somehow, but he was long since dead as of the Civil War." And that's true. But in this case, I'll need to tell you where we're headed in order to make the most sense of where we've been.

It's 1861. And a new nation—not yet even a century old—is fracturing from within. Cannonballs begin to fly. Previously "United" States begin to secede by the week. Sons and brothers and fathers leave families behind as they march toward peril. Supply routes are cut off.

As might be expected, panic ensues.

In their dismay, people begin to hoard items of value— including coins, many of which, at the time, were made of gold and silver. As the war raged on, even cents began to be stashed away on account of the semi-precious metal nickel which they contained. And this frenzy resulted in an ever-dwindling supply of currency in circulation.

As a result, local businesses, figuring the federal government had much bigger fish to fry, began paying to have *their own store currency* made and circulated— made from cheap metals to avoid the hoarding craze, and conveniently the same size and shape as the federally-minted one-cent piece. Before long, store patrons began to cash them in.

And so it was that the first Civil War token entered the economy.

But soon, these tokens began to show up at other flailing stores—the owners of which either didn't notice or simply said, "Eh, what the heck" and so also began to accept them as payment. In fact, this "personal currency" system worked so well that other large businesses began commissioning their own unique private stashes of tokens to be made. Within just two years, about 25 million such Civil War tokens had flooded the mainstream, consisting of as many as 8,000 different varieties.

The Coinage Act of 1864 finally put the kibosh on these

tokens, threatening imprisonment and fines up to 200,000 times the value of the coins. However, before that move is where Ben Franklin finally comes into the story. You see, the image of Benjamin Franklin appeared on the heads side of one of those myriad Civil War tokens. And on the tails side was imprinted "★ PENNY SAVED IS A PENNY EARNED" (where the star is presumably a patriotic graphic substitution for "A"). *This*, then, is the first time the current iteration of the phrase turns up in English.

By the same token (I couldn't resist), it is also how the rumor began that Ben Franklin himself coined (there I go again) the phrase.

Well, if he *wasn't* the first to give us this wording of the old adage, how did the Civil War token bearing his likeness come to wind up with *that* particular saying on the back? As it happens, Benjamin Franklin *had* famously given us a version of it some 125 years earlier, wrapped in such sound financial wisdom that *Forbes* still cites it to this day as some of the best practical advice ever offered on the subject of money.

You surely associate Ben Franklin with the U.S. $100 bill. Perhaps you envision him flying a key at the end of a kite whilst playing with lightning; or leaning over a desk, his self-made bifocals perched on the end of his nose, drafting or signing the Declaration of Independence. There's no doubt that Franklin was a Renaissance man. But what many don't know—or have merely forgotten—is that he was also a famous writer. Using the pen name "Richard Saunders," Franklin wrote the famed *Poor Richard's Almanack* (as originally spelled), which published annually for 25 years.

In his fifth issue, published in 1737—nestled between poetry, eclipse predictions and an antidote for rattlesnake bites—Franklin included a short piece called "Hints for those that would be Rich." And it is at the conclusion of this article that Franklin paraphrased the original maxim:

A Penny sav'd is Twopence clear...

Being a well-read man (and, in fact, a founder of the first subscription library in the colonies), Franklin would most certainly have been familiar with George Herbert's collection. But the majority of the population would as certainly *not* have had a clue who Herbert was. And so it becomes understandable how this piece of **tried-and-(still)-true** wisdom became attributed to the American hero who brought it home to his generation with such vivid clarity.

......

Time for some trivia—both about the history of pennies and about the image I chose for the cover of this book.

You probably know that the mainstay of British currency is the pound. What you may not have known, however, is that until relatively recently, British currency was not based on divisions of ten or five like the American dollar, but rather on divisions of 20 and 12. That is, there were 240 pennies or "pence" in a sterling pound. One shilling was 1/20th of a pound. And one penny was 1/12th of a shilling, though the pre-decimalization penny was substantially larger than its American counterpart—about the size of a U.S. half dollar.

One might have been confused by its symbol, "d" (e.g., sixpence was written "6d") without knowing that it hailed from the ancient Roman coin known as the denarius, the use of which ended by the third century A.D. But while the British "old penny" was retired on Decimal Day (February 15, 1971), the word denarius lives on in other countries as *denaro* (Italian "money"), *dinero* (Spanish "money") and others.

Now, I frequently hear Americans carping about how they wish the federal government would do away with the U.S. penny altogether, usually adding "they're so annoying." I disagree. However, I'd love to see these same people's reactions to the British coinage system up through the 1960s, in which the penny was not the runt of coins. There was also a half penny or "ha'penny" (pronounced "HAY-penny"). And half of *that* was a farthing (e.g., a quarter penny, "farth" being from the same root we get "fourth").

Anyway, if you're one of those people who's annoyed with pennies nowadays, try having been the person standing in line at the convenience store behind the guy who's paying his one-pound total by counting out 960 farthings.

Here's a little more history on the penny. Ever wonder why the United States has *two* words for its smallest coin: "penny" and "cent"? I mean, there aren't two different words for a nickel or dime or quarter. So why single one coin out for the extra moniker? Well, that English penny obviously made the journey to The Americas with the early settlers. After the Revolutionary War, however, unique currency with its own system began to be commissioned. In fact, the very first currency minted in the States, commissioned by George Washington himself, was the "one-cent piece."

While the origin of the word "penny" isn't exactly clear, the use of pennies goes back to about 790 A.D., though using slightly different names such as *pfenning* (Germany) and *penning* (Sweden). But "cent" comes to us from the Latin for "hundred." Just as a *century* is 100 years or *percent* means "for each 100," the one-cent piece came to mean that 100 of them made up a dollar. And while breaking things up this way may seem normal to *you*, try to empathize with early Americans who'd only ever known that size coin to represent 1/240th. After all, the new American coin was modeled after the English penny—about five times the weight and twice the size of today's US one-cent coin. Sure, it *looked* a little different, but old habits die hard; and so people continued to use the more familiar term "penny," despite the words imprinted on their new copper coins.

And now, for the inside scoop I promised regarding the illustration I chose for the cover of this book.

When I settled upon lemonade as the cover image for my last book, *The Best Advice So Far*, I can't tell you the number of people who said, "It feels inviting… but why *lemonade*?" Then they'd get to Chapter 39, entitled "Lemonade," and it would all make sense.

With *Tried & (Still) True*, however, the connection may not be as apparent. The original art depicts three small bugs also riding bikes behind our frog—two on a tandem bicycle (well, one is flying off the back) and one riding a unicycle. However, these tiny companions didn't seem to add to the central theme I was going for, and so they were edited out of the cover image (though you'll notice them elsewhere in the book).

The bicycle that the frog is riding, on the other hand, *does* have significance. And now that you've got a brief history of the penny and the farthing under your belt, you can likely make a fair guess as to why Mr. Frog's bicycle was named the *penny farthing*. If it's still not apparent, not only was the farthing's worth smaller than that of the penny, the farthing itself was noticeably smaller at about two-thirds the size of the penny—just as the front wheel of the penny farthing bicycle is substantially larger than its back wheel.

Of course, the name of the bicycle was just an additional fun factoid. As I considered the title of this book and its premise—before I'd even written a single word—*Frog on a Penny Farthing* captured both my imagination and the vibe I was going for. Times have changed, but *principles* have not. A penny farthing, as outdated as it may appear to modern eyes, still *works*. Likewise, the wisdom in this book, while increasingly unfamiliar to contemporary ears, is just as reliable as ever it was.

And in case you were wondering, *Why the frog?*... I felt it would pique curiosity, as well as convey that *old* doesn't automatically mean *boring*.

(*Still*) **TRUE**

I would be doing you a disservice if I didn't start this section by providing for you at least some of the article from that 1737 issue of *Poor Richard's Almanack*, as penned by

Benjamin Franklin himself. Before I do, however, a short glossary will help:

> **5s.**: 5 shillings
>
> **groat**: four pennies; a small sum
>
> **mickle**: a large sum or amount
>
> **pin**: a trifling amount; a farthing
>
> **ready money**: cash; readily available money

And now for Franklin's uncannily ageless advice. It's a bit tricky in places, but spend some time with it. I promise, it'll be worth the effort.

Hints for those that would be Rich.

The Use of Money is all the Advantage there is in having Money...

He that wastes idly a Groat's worth of his Time per Day, one Day with another, wastes the Privilege of using £100 each Day.

He that idly loses 5s. worth of time, loses 5s. and might as prudently throw 5s. in the River...

Consider then, when you are tempted to buy any unnecessary Housholdstuff, or any superfluous thing, whether you will be willing to pay Interest, and Interest upon Interest for it as long as you live; and more if it grows worse by using.

Yet, in buying Goods, 'tis best to pay ready Money, because,

He that sells upon Credit, expects to lose 5 per Cent. by bad Debts; therefore he charges, on all he sells upon Credit, an Advance that shall make up that Deficiency.

Those who pay for what they buy upon Credit, pay their Share of this Advance.

He that pays ready Money, escapes or may escape that Charge.

A Penny sav'd is Twopence clear, A Pin a day is a Groat a Year. Save and have. Every little makes a mickle.

Let me bring those Pins and Groats home with a true story about how I gave myself a sizable annual raise. I'm not the CEO of a big company. Nor am I a shyster. I don't trade in Bitcoin. Truth be told, I don't actually make any more money now than before the raise. Nonetheless, I wound up with about $3,000 a year in additional money at my disposal going forward than I would have had as of just a few short weeks prior.

Have I got you sufficiently mystified? Good. Now let me share my secret…

I cut caffeine.

Yup, that's it. I cut one small but constant siphon out of my life and *voila!* I was suddenly richer, and by a hefty sum. That same year, I took a nice extended vacation, and $3,000 is actually a little *more* than I paid to stay six full weeks in a luxury home with a club, gym, pools, waterfalls—even its own private theater. That *includes* airfare.

My decision to ditch caffeine was primarily for the health benefits. But honestly, it was those few tippety-taps on the calculator that sealed the deal—because I realized I was spending roughly *eight dollars a day for something I didn't need.*

The funny thing is, I'd been in that cycle for more than three years. I knew what each individual caffeine product cost (those "Pins" Franklin talks about)—and yet the cumulative amount I was paying annually never once occurred to me. If someone had told me at the start, "Hey, I know a guaranteed way you can bank an extra $10,000 over the next three years with no extra work involved," I would have assumed it was a pyramid scheme. And yet it turns out that my superfluous caffeine drinks actually did make me ten grand poorer during that time period. As Ben put it, "Every little makes a mickle."

In the same way, you can get an instant 50% savings or greater on just about anything, anytime you want. All you need to do… is use half as much.

No, really. We've become accustomed to letting sales-driven companies and their marketing teams tell us how much of their products we need, instead of using our own judgment regarding portion size. Most restaurant plates served for one could easily be the makings of *two* meals—one now and one later. Will swishing half as much mouthwash really work less? (While we're on the subject of those marketers and their wily ways, did you know that Listerine mouthwash execs *invented* the word "halitosis" to make bad breath sound like a medical problem, just so that they could sell more of their product to "cure" it?) And while many paper towel brands now perforate to allow for half-sheet tears, who's to say that even that much is necessary for every job? For instance, when I use dry-eye drops, do I really need a half-sheet to dab my eyes afterward? I find that tearing off a fourth (farthing?) of that half-sheet is plenty for the purpose at hand. That's a quarter of half of a sheet. Just think of all the pennies saved, and thus earned.

As I did with my caffeine products, try adding up what you think you spend on paper towels in a year and then cut the amount in half. That's the amount you *could* be saving—and spending on something *else*.

I just asked my mother (who, you'll recall, is an expert in parsimony) how much she thinks she spends on paper towels in a year. Buying in bulk and shopping at discount stores, she *still* estimates that she spends nearly $200 a year on this one household product. So let's say you're as frugal as my mom (you're not, but let's suppose for now). Half that amount would be $100 per year you could be saving for something else you *really* want. Six or seven books? Money toward a plane ticket? Your retirement fund?

Obviously, this is about more than paper towels. I'm talking about allowing "a penny saved is a penny earned" to become a mindset, a lifestyle. On a whim, I took a look at the "instructions" on the bottle of a popular brand of shampoo from the shower of the vacation home where I'd been enjoying a break. OK, first—do we really need instructions for shampoo? Be that as it may, the full paragraph of instructions starts thusly: "Coat hair with a *liberal amount* of [our product]." But I ask you, what apocalyptic horrors do you suppose might befall you if you used (dare I say it?) a *sensible* amount of shampoo—just enough to get that squeak from your hair that says it's clean?

Or if you usually make 10 swipes per armpit with your deodorant, how badly do you think life would go for you and those around you if you used, say, only 5 or 6? *Every little makes a mickle.* I'm not talking about skimping. I'm talking about using no more than you really *need.* Don't think of it in terms of deprivation—what you *don't* get. Think of it in terms of those "pennies earned" that will give you *more* freedom to enjoy other things of greater value to you.

I'm convinced that another reason people are reluctant to save pennies is that they're worried about what other people will think. In "The Gift of the Magi," we see Della's "cheeks burning" in embarrassment at her attempts to save her pennies for a Christmas gift; and such stories find a lasting place largely because of our ability to relate, at least on some level. Think about it, though. Why do we feel "less than" if the person behind us in the grocery line sees us handing over clipped coupons? Why do we imagine that house guests will look down their noses at us if we buy generic hand soap or tissues rather than the name brands? Or why do we pass over that dime we notice in the convenience store parking lot if we see someone else approaching or leaving, when we'd otherwise have picked it up?

Allow me to take a short detour that will lead back to the point at hand.

There are many hobbies and habits I've had since I was very young. Playing the piano. Singing. Reading voraciously. If you haven't noticed, kids can be mean. As such, I was teased, taunted—even bullied—over some of these pursuits. And it would have been easier in many ways to just bend to the pressure. Give in for the sake of popularity, or at least to avoid the torment. But I didn't. I stuck out my chin and stuck to my guns.

Well, another longstanding daily practice of mine has been using facial moisturizer, which I started when I was a teen. People gossiped about it. I got called some not-so-nice names. "I hear you use *girl* stuff," one classmate gibed. I endured it and kept right on using that moisturizer.

You may be wondering what all of this has got to do with the saving of pennies. Well, if I'd lived my life and made my choices based on other people's opinions at every turn, I'd have missed out on the joy and comfort and creative outlet that music has been throughout a lifetime. Yes, some "temporary people" from the past laughed and poked fun, but they lacked foresight. Within a few short years, by the time I went off to college, my ability to play the piano, sing and write music was considered cool, envied even. There was no jeering when I was able to make $200 an hour playing for wedding receptions or when I released my first album.

And decades later, I'm here to tell you that none of those old acquaintances are laughing now about my moisturizing regimen. That's all I'll say about that.

Similarly, we all have "temporary people"—those customers behind us in line at the grocer's as we consider whether or not to use our coupons, the patron exiting the QuickMart when we see that free dime on the lot—whose opinions (real or imagined) about our commitment to saving and earning pennies *don't matter. Your* pennies saved are *your* pennies earned. Your "littles" are *your* future "mickles," not theirs. Believe in yourself, your choices, your purpose and your plan. I picked up a useful saying from a friend, one I've repeated often whenever I or someone I'm with is tempted to alter our course based on possible opinions from others. It's a tongue-in-cheek quip, but it's also got truth to it: "They ain't payin' *my* bills. So who cares what they think?" Trust me—no one will be laughing when you don't have debt, or when you head off on that vacation you were able to save for, or when you start cashing out your Roth IRA. Even in the short run, if someone wants to arch an eyebrow at me for stooping to pick up a coin, let 'em. The change bag of found money that I keep in the armrest compartment of my car is so full, it recently ripped when I tried to retrieve it, and I had to replace it. That change has paid for everything from tire air to bottled drinks to ice cream treats on a steady basis. So who's the fool?

Saving pennies isn't just about paying less or cutting back. It's just as often about restraint. Buying "stuff" is often not about what we *need* at all. If we're not careful, we can fall into the trap of buying out of sheer habit. Or because we're feeling pressured or boxed in elsewhere, and buying gives us a temporary sense of release. Or because we've developed a mindset of dissatisfaction or pride that drives us to have *the newest or best* gadgets, even when the ones we have work perfectly fine.

I have one young cousin who was struggling to pay his

basic bills when he was forced to move out on his own after his mom died. He never seemed to have money, despite having a steady job that paid fairly well for his age, and having government assistance for everything from housing to utilities to food. I sat him down for an honest conversation to see where the paychecks were disappearing to. After a half-hour of progressive questioning, he admitted in utter embarrassment that he'd spent $60 already that month on shoes. Not shoes he needed. Not even shoes for himself. In fact, not even shoes *for a real person*. He'd spent $60 of his *actual* money to buy various sneakers for his player in one of his go-to basketball video games. That's right: this fake character was running around with expensive new digital footwear, while the flesh-and-blood young man who created him didn't have the money left to keep his phone in service or to eat properly. And as I asked the even deeper questions, it became clear to us both that this strange compulsion was undergirded by a deep sense of loss and an irrational attempt to restore a sense of control. And yet, clearly, this coping strategy was self-defeating. He was causing twice the anxiety by way of threatening calls from bill collectors or an empty stomach than he was relieving with his momentary (and meaningless) splurging.

I have other friends who feel a palpable sense of anxiety if they aren't among the first to pre-order the next version of their phone months in advance. Marketers pander to such people by referring to them as "trendsetters" or "influencers." This flattering terminology serves their purpose of transferring lots of consumers' "pennies earned" into "pennies lost" (or, rather, conveniently transferred to themselves). And why not, when they can charge hundreds of dollars more by targeting this group than they'll be able to get for the same device next quarter?

Again, I'm not decrying treating yourself to nicer things. I'm simply advocating for careful consideration of *why* we're buying them in the first place. Why this? Why *now*?

When it comes to extras, see what happens if you implement a new rule: "If I still think I need this in three days, I'll get it." Often, even the most minimal delay brings clarity, helping us to avoid pitfalls that pilfer our pennies—whether two by two, or by the bagful.

Not **TRUE**

I want to reiterate here at the start of this section that "A penny saved is a penny earned" isn't necessarily about forced austerity or deprivation. Sometimes it is, as was the case during the Great Depression or even periods of my own upbringing. I myself have already mentioned taking extended vacations. I replace my laptop every few years. I own a nice set of noise-cancelling headphones I use while writing out in public. But I can afford these things *because* I've saved my pennies and thus *earned* these extras. I spend time seeking the best deal on the vacations and wind up paying about a quarter of the list price; and I got my last new laptop at less than half the original price by simply putting a watch on it and then *waiting* until it was about to be discontinued (which, at the rate new technology rolls out, was only about six months after it was released). So I assure you, I'm not sitting home in my hovel by the light of one candle, eating my rations of bread crusts and water. I'm living just fine. Enjoying life. Having fun. I'm just doing it with "ready money" instead of on credit—using lots of pennies saved elsewhere.

It's not just about saving for the occasional big-ticket items, either. For me, it's about choosing to find joy in little things. A walk on the beach at sunset is free, immersive entertainment. So is a conversation with a good person. The relatively small amount it costs to buy a book can provide hours of enjoyment over the course of days or weeks (and if you borrow the book from a library, that too is free). Even at my age, I've never gotten over the thrill and feeling of freedom that comes with buying a 99-cent soft-serve ice cream cone on a hot summer day. If we can detach our contentment with or enjoyment of things from their price tags, the penny-saving possibilities are endless.

To supplement this chapter's **tried-and-(still)-true** saying with a tidbit of modern wisdom:

> *"Be thankful for what you have; you'll end up having more. If you concentrate on what you don't have, you will never, ever have enough."* — **Oprah Winfrey**

If you're doing it right, saving pennies should never feel like drudgery. Look at it as a fun challenge, something like hunting for that elusive piece of a jigsaw puzzle, or finding Waldo. New ways to save your pennies are always there; it's up to you to be perceptive enough to spot them when others can't. My mom absolutely instilled in me that sense of gamification where thrift is concerned. "Guess how much I paid for this *entire* stack of clothes!" she'll call out after returning from a garage sale, holding up each piece for our inspection. "This is perfectly good, brand-name stuff!"

She once waltzed in with a beautiful Tiffany lamp she picked up for free at some frou-frou gallery after noticing the proprietor had broken a panel from the lead and was ready to discard it. "Please don't throw it away," she'd said. "I think I can fix it." And once home, she'd carefully replaced the cracked glass, glued the seam and simply turned that small flaw toward the wall. I can't tell you how many compliments she got on that lamp over the years.

She never talked about what she spent on food shopping, only what she *saved.*

When she's done reading a book, she turns it in at a local used-book seller for half the cover value in credit toward more books.

To this day, I don't think she's ever purchased an item by any means that was full price; and she still revels in announcing the list price as compared with what she paid (which is rarely more than half retail).

My mother learned these values from her parents. However, while my mom applied them at first out of necessity and later for the personal satisfaction of it, my grandparents had a different motivation: *fear*. Having both been born in the early 1920s, their formative years were shaped by the Great Depression, when even things as simple as having a next meal were not guaranteed. Then came World War II. And so they lived simply. Yet while my Nana always kept a tidy home, both she and my Grampa battled against hoarding tendencies. If there was an unbelievable sale on necessities such as toilet paper or light bulbs, they bought the whole lot of them and stockpiled them in the basement.

Yet as the years passed, that basement became full to the brim with yellowed and molded toilet paper that had wicked up decades of flood water, light bulbs that had long since corroded right through their boxes, and dozens of other essentials they'd "saved big" on at the time the items were purchased.

I trust the irony is not lost. Fear-based living almost always leads to waste eventually.

Still, my grandparents *also* exemplified that thrift is not the same as miserliness. As I mentioned earlier, no matter how poor they were, Nana and Grampa always managed to tuck a $10 bill into each grandkid's birthday card. It was only many years later that I truly grasped the magnitude of that sacrifice. And somehow, they hosted family gatherings on the regular, feeding thirty-some-odd people at a time with endless flounder Grampa had pulled from the ocean himself for free and cooked up in a simple batter of flour, butter, salt and pepper. They were masters of delivering extravagance on a shoestring.

Even with their basement full of wares, it was never just for themselves. If any of their children or grandchildren so much as mentioned being out of something, they'd say, "I think there are some in the cellar. Take them."

Allow me another example of when *not* to worry about your pennies: *tipping*. I recall a certain afternoon some years back when I joined some "church ladies" for lunch. There were perhaps eight of us in total. They were picky and changed their minds often. Then, after an hour and a half of special requests, they asked the server for separate checks. Once these were delivered (with a smile, I might add), the ladies began to literally dump their change out on the table and slide nickels and pennies out, counting them aloud until they reached 15%... rounding *down* a penny, of course. One of them did attempt to simply leave three dollar bills; but with pursed lips, another woman from the gaggle snatched one from the small pile and tucked it into her pocketbook. "Oh, that's *way* too much," she chided with knit brows. She then proceeded to dole out thirteen cents to add to the tip, and handed her friend eighty-seven cents back.

I'll be blunt. Not only was this rude, it didn't speak well of their church or purported beliefs.

After we all parted ways, I marched back in, found the server, and handed her another $10 bill with an apologetic smile and some light-hearted remark about how it's tough to get old. Thing is, those ladies weren't *that* old.

I'd recommend that if you can't afford to tip or don't intend to, *don't eat out*. Saving one's pennies should never come at the expense of generosity. I'm talking about a dollar or two here. You'll never miss it. But to a server, that extra dollar and the percentage it represents is often the difference between feeling appreciated—or exasperated. Sometimes, it's even the reason a server can pay rent on time.

Always keep at the forefront that *people* are more important than *money*, and you'll seldom go wrong.

By the way, "A penny saved is a penny earned" doesn't just apply to poor people or those struggling to make ends meet. Choosing to live mindfully—even simply—has countless benefits, regardless of one's level of wealth. An ongoing Harvard study that's been in progress for more than 80 years reports that over a certain amount, reported "happiness" scores don't change much. The same study found that *earning* money makes people feel significantly happier than having it fall on them by inheritance, marriage or lottery; and that *giving money away*, to benefit a person or cause, brings more happiness than spending it on oneself.

Another study out of UCLA backs this up. It reveals that buying "stuff"—particularly for oneself—results in substantially less happiness than spending money to free up time, to enjoy shared experiences or to help someone else.

My point in introducing the studies is to say that just because you *can* buy whatever you like any time you have the whim doesn't mean you *should*.

Though not the focal point of this chapter, it seems a good time to introduce another noteworthy pearl of **tried-and-(still)-true** wisdom:

"Necessity is the mother of invention."

If we indulge every urge that our money can fulfill, we lose much more than pennies. We chisel away at parts of ourselves that are difficult to regain, not the least of which is creativity. I can't easily recount the number of useful—even highly profitable—skills I've learned over the years, during stretches when money was tighter than I'd have liked. I'd never have released my first book when I did if I'd had to rely on paying others the thousands necessary to complete different phases of the project. So in order to reach my goals, I wound up expanding my creative toolbox, one which had already been started and added to through earlier periods of scarcity: navigation of self-publishing platforms, cover design, print layout, e-book programming, specifics of audiobook recording and editing; and more.

Today, though I *can* afford such "extras," I still prefer the inspiration, autonomy and sense of personal challenge that comes with doing things with a good helping of tenacity and my own two hands.

Similarly, I don't think I'd have learned how to cook if I could always have afforded to eat out or order in.

Furthermore, how can we hope to develop the quality of patience if we never have to wait for anything? How do we learn contentment if enough is never actually *enough*? And where patience and contentment wane, any number of less savory qualities are all too eager to take their place: intolerance, selfishness, indifference.

Google "Why aren't millionaires happy?" and you'll find more than three-quarters of a million results. The tales of lottery winners who become depressed, even suicidal, *after* their windfall are so common as to have become clichéd. And a familiar refrain among them is that once they could do anything they liked and no longer had to *dream* and *imagine*—something inside of them died. Ironically, it seems, when everything is within our reach, nothing any longer feels special. The cautionary tale, then, is that if the end goal is peace, happiness and fulfillment, continual spending for the sake of spending won't get you there.

Finally, consider that saving and earning doesn't apply

solely to our pennies. Benjamin Franklin also pointed out in that 1737 edition of *Poor Richard's Almanack* that, essentially, "Time is money"—an observation which he would coin just over a decade later in these exact words ("Advice to a Young Tradesman," 1748). Like money, time can be spent, squandered or lost. However, unlike money, time can never be *gained or accumulated*, making it an even more valuable commodity. As such, time devoted to one area is immediately *lost* to all other pursuits.

If you're already familiar with this quote, I'd challenge you to not only read it again or even to nod your head and agree, but to consider it anew, however you choose to do that.

A friend of mine, Chad, shared with me a contemporary piece of wisdom, one I haven't been able to shake since hearing it:

> **Instead of saying "I don't have time" or "I'm too busy," try saying "That's not a priority for me."**

Whether you happen to have heard this before or not, take this opportunity to really think about it in relation to your own recent choices. Perhaps write it down and focus on it for a day, or discuss it with a positive person in your life.

I don't know about you, but my initial reaction to this felt like being woken from a sound sleep and having my head plunged into a bucket of ice water.

I wanted to say, "That's just motivational mumbo-jumbo that sounds cool."

I wanted to say, "No, that's not really true. Look, here's an example."

Thing is, I couldn't really come up with a legitimate counter. Even, say, missing your daughter's dance recital due to work doesn't earn a free pass here. Working those hours, making that money, keeping that job... were the priority over going to the dance recital. It's as simple and economical as that. This wouldn't be to say that you don't love your daughter or that you don't support her in dance; but by its very nature, it *does* say that the job/time/money were more important than being at the recital. And that may be a perfectly reasonable and sound decision.

Or not.

Only you know the truth about where your time is spent and what that indicates about your priorities. And only I know that about my own choices, about the difference between priorities set by true need—and priorities motivated by something else entirely:

> ... like that Pavlovian feeling of uneasiness unless we keep the powerful or emotionally draining people appeased at all times (at the expense of considering those who can't give us something back or who don't complain quite so loudly).

> ... like the never-ending quest for status or position.

> ... like a focus on material things over personal relationships.

> ... like failure to consider the things that are

important to people other than myself.

... like failure to consider other people *at all*.

For me, I realized that my struggle at that particular time was actually considering *myself*—my own time and my own goals—as a priority.

It wasn't an obvious thing. I wasn't walking around feeling "less than." But when aligned against what Chad presented about "too busy" meaning "not a priority," my own choices as to what I'd been taking on in life revealed that the thing I'd been too busy to spend time on... was *me*.

I'd gotten into a habit of essentially saying,

> "Your time is a higher priority than my own time."

> "Your goals and dreams are a higher priority than my own goals and dreams."

> "Your happiness is a higher priority than my own happiness."

And if I'm being completely honest here, there's something about those statements that feels somehow *right*. It feels righteous and good.

It's utter rubbish, of course; but it *feels* like it should be true—that good people, *nice* people, ought to think this way.

I know the truth. And that is not truth, however "right" it feels based on past dysfunction in our lives. However "right" other people may tell us it is. However noble they may tell us we are when we live this way (especially, I've noticed, when they are hoping to become my priority at the moment).

In my first book, *The Best Advice So Far*, I included three chapters centered on advice passed along to me by my friend Carlotta. But those three weren't the only keepers. Perhaps her shortest is a gem in keeping with "A penny saved…":

"Save yourself!"

Carlotta's daughter (and my best friend) Dib is kind enough to remind me of this one often, usually followed by, "My mother was brilliant." I concur. Those two simple words have helped right my ship countless times.

Now, I'll be direct. The tendency to continually prioritize others over oneself is certainly not *everyone's* pitfall. And if it's not yours, you know this. So don't misuse this pithy prescription to justify a continued modus operandi of self-centeredness. But if this does ring true for you, remind yourself often that if you don't "save yourself," you will be in no position to help anyone else. As our kindly flight attendants instruct, "Place the mask securely over your own mouth before assisting others."

As with most things in life, making wise choices regarding how we spend both our money and our time comes down to balance.

Questions & A Challenge

1. How do you think your own upbringing has affected your relationship with money and spending?

2. Are there any emotional or mental "side-effects," good or bad, that you believe can result from being money conscious? How about from *not* being money conscious?

3. What is your reaction to this statement: "*Instead of saying 'I don't have time' or 'I'm too busy,' try saying 'That's not a priority for me.'*"? What might your own choices regarding how you spend your time be saying about your priorities?

CHALLENGE: Choose one non-essential item that you buy regularly and calculate an estimate of how much you spend on that item annually. What else could you be doing with that lump sum of money? As an experiment, try cutting out the item you chose for a single week, keeping note of the cumulative savings daily. At the end of your experiment, put that amount of money toward something else (e.g., spend it on an immediate "treat," add it to a special savings account, put it in a vacation jar, etc.). You earned it!

6

waste

ONE SPRING several years back, I found myself looking into a little side gig as a content editor for a startup out of New York. It seemed a good deal at first: ten flex hours at the rate I requested. The owner was desperate. Before ending that Friday afternoon phone call, they were pleading with me to edit three articles over Memorial Day weekend.

There I was, money on the table so to speak, being pressed for an immediate answer. So without further consideration, I accepted on the spot. I figured I could handle it once I was in the door and through the initial messiness. Mind my own business. Do what I agreed to do. Collect my paycheck.

Not so.

It changed. It grew. Heck, it mutated.

Not having given myself space to vet this company properly, I noticed in that first set of "emergency" articles that some of the claims and statistics just didn't seem plausible. So I checked the sources and, sure enough, the data being reported was off. I mean *way* off. Not even close to what the article was purporting. I thought, *If a client ever saw this number of egregious errors, they'd drop this company in a heartbeat!*

I alerted the boss.

She asked me to fix it "just this once."

A week in, and I was asked last-minute if I could "just

bail them out on a few things" due to a writer who'd had a baby and left several articles half-done.

This seemed reasonable given the circumstances, so I went ahead and said I'd bail them out.

Meanwhile, the majority of articles I was continuing to edit were pure garbage. Honest to Pete, they read like a sixth-grader had written them (and not a particularly astute one at that). It quickly became standard fare for me to have to slash 80% of the copy—which, of course, was taking much, *much* longer than agreed upon. As much as *ten times longer*, in fact.

I pointed out to the owner that *most* of the articles I was given to edit were now not only poorly written, fluffy, off-topic or illogical—but misinterpretation (or misrepresentation) of supporting research was rampant. I reminded her that we'd agreed that writing and proper inclusion of credible support data was the writers' job, not mine. My pay rate was supposed to be following word-count brackets based on those clear expectations. I was to edit as I saw fit. I was not required to explain my edits. I was not required to read source articles or fact check.

The owner responded with snippy and condescending remarks. I reflected back to her how she was coming across, despite the fact that I was now "bailing her out" constantly. She returned, "Well, it's a little tiring having you continue to come to me and ask me why you have to do this or that, or telling me that it's the writers' job. This is a startup. The lines blur. So the reason you should do what I tell you to do is *because I said so*. I shouldn't have to explain myself to you."

By the six-month point, I was being *expected* to

"coach" all of the writers (i.e., to leave copious comments regarding reasons for my edits along with suggestions for how they could fix things, though none of the writers ever applied the learning to the next article). I was also now being required to read all of the linked articles and verify all stats for accuracy, to find *new and valid* data to replace slipshod research, and to work that into the articles myself.

My initial generous offer of a few days' turnaround on articles somehow turned into a mandatory 24 hours. Then 12.

I was now putting in 25 or more hours a week... yet somehow only getting paid for 3 or 4 hours, based on the initial word-count agreement.

When I expressed mounting frustrations and concerns, they were ignored, as if I hadn't spoken at all.

My own personal writing pursuits had taken a back burner to the new and ever-growing drudgery and stress of editing material I didn't care about.

I was staying up until 4:00 or 5:00 AM to complete edits on articles containing shoddy copy that never improved.

I was missing the gym often at this point, which made me feel even worse.

My stomach was in knots.

And it was leaking over into my personal life and conversations with others, so distracted was I at how horrible it all had become.

December rolled in. It was Christmas time—and I was missing it.

I made one last effort to communicate my concerns and frustrations to the owner. I spent about an hour carefully putting into words just how I'd been feeling and sent it to her through the private messaging app. The message showed as "Read." But by way of reply... I got radio silence. The articles kept coming my way, but my heartfelt personal message was never addressed—or even acknowledged.

Three days later, I gave a four-week notice. I was told to leave in 10 days—one final slap as if to say, "You're really not all that hard to replace, you know." (Though within a week, she was back on my digital doorstep, asking ever so politely, with big blinky eyes, if I might bail her out just once more and only on a handful of articles, "just until we narrow down our final search for a new editor." I declined.)

On New Year's Eve, at long last, I was free of it.

But all I could think when that moment came was...
What a colossal waste of six months.

Now, the reasons I stayed as long as I did given the chaos and ill treatment are a matter I discuss at length in *The Best Advice So Far*, in a chapter devoted to what I call **B.E.A.S.T.s** (**B**ig **E**nergy-**A**bsorbing **S**tupid **T**hings). But as for why I ever got involved with this awful situation *in the first place*, that I can address rather easily and with utmost clarity.

The fact is, nearly every bad decision I can remember making has been the result of not having taken enough time to consider and weigh the potential consequences of what I was getting myself into.

TRIED

Haste makes waste.

My first book, *The Best Advice So Far*, is a collection of sorts. After 25 years of mentoring, it seemed a natural next step. I'd just gained so many useful pieces of wisdom from various people and places across a lifetime "so far" that passing them on verbally to one or two people at a time felt limited. Even selfish somehow. And so I began the process of writing them down in one place, nestled among essays and stories from my own life and times. When it felt complete, I shared it with the world in print.

As it so happens, here I am writing yet *another* collection, and for similar reasons.

Well, it seems the same kind of notion began to gnaw at a guy named John Heywood. In fact, he was just about my age when he committed to penning his second of such collections (though his title may not have been as snappy as my own):

A Dialogue Conteinyng the Nomber in Effect of All the Prouerbes in the Englishe Tongue, Compacte in a Matter Concernyng Two Maner of Mariages

Note the irony that the word "compact" appears in this title.

For those who start to hyperventilate at anything approximating your high school English teacher making you read the original texts of Shakespeare, here's what the title might have looked like if John had released it today instead of in 1546:

All the Proverbs I've Heard About Marriage

Understand that, like me, John Heywood made no claim to have been the *originator* of the advice found in his books. He just felt compelled that *someone* ought to record in one written volume what was, in his day, being preserved only by word of mouth. And it's a good thing he *did*. For while his works seem quite old to us today, the actual wisdom they contain was considered old even in *his* day—so old, in fact, that no one will ever know who first uttered any of it. That is to say that, without John Heywood's dedication to the task, a whole lot of solid wisdom would surely have been lost forever.

Similarly, my aim in writing *Tried & (Still) True* was to introduce a new generation to real wisdom that we as a culture are collectively forgetting once again. But even for those readers who *are* old enough to have grown up hearing "Haste makes waste," I'd venture to guess that it wasn't in regard to *marriage*. Yet the full context in which these words appear makes the intent clear beyond doubt. Here it is as originally written:

> **Som thyngs that prouoke yong men to wed in haste**
> **Show after weddyng that haste maketh waste.**

Now, before everyone over 50 gets to feeling like you were hoodwinked as a child by teachers and parents who cited "Haste makes waste" as a reprimand for poor penmanship or racing through chores, it turns out Heywood covered that ground with a similar proverb, one we'll dive into a little further on.

...&...

In many ways, "Haste makes waste" is a perfect proverb. Like "Know thyself" (Chapter 1), it qualifies as an aphorism. That is, its brevity actually allows it to have *broader* application than if it had tried to be more specific and wordy. Again, like art or music, it is open to *many* interpretations, in this case depending on the context, the speaker and the listener. And so while various interpretations may differ from one another, they may also each be absolutely *true* and thus equally valuable.

Each word of this saying is a single syllable in length. Yet even in those three short words, the saying manages to include rhythm and rhyme in "Mary-had-a-little-lamb" fashion. And that means it just begs to be *said*. This all makes it memorable—or in modern terminology, *brandable*. And that's good news for those of us who sincerely want to *apply* wisdom in ways that matter. Like a catchy jingle, just let the words roll off your tongue a few times and they'll be yours for life.

(Still) TRUE

With regard to Heywood's marital context of our central saying, I suspect that a good number of those "things that provoke young men to wed in haste" haven't changed much in 500 years. What's more, the waste that occurs from jumping into (or out of) relationships without careful consideration—emotional upheaval, divorce, financial loss, children caught in the fray—are certainly as evident today as ever before.

Strangely enough, while "Haste makes waste" was first associated with marriage, the meaning most popularly attributed to the words at the turn of the twentieth century was *also* covered by a rather similar inclusion in another of Heywood's collections:

The more haste, the less speed.

And this *did*, in fact, essentially mean what we older lot were told: that rushing sloppily through a task usually results in needing to redo it later—thus causing us to spend more time and effort on it than if we'd done it properly in the first place.

For those younger readers who are just now getting acquainted with "Haste makes waste," and who therefore may never have thought much about this concept, let's take a closer look. (And let's be honest: even those of us who grew up with it could benefit from a refresher.)

At the most basic level, what is meant here is that hurrying lends itself to a higher incidence of physical error. No one cautions children: "Don't walk with scissors." It's the *running* that's the potential problem.

Think about it. How many times have you found your-self running late and tried to race through your morning routine, only to suddenly find yourself tending to bleeding nicks from shaving; or unable to hold onto a bar of soap; or growling in irritation on your hands and knees as you try to find the last of the pills you sent skittering across the kitchen floor?

Or you've got four bags of groceries, a backpack, a sweater, keys, phone and a coffee to get out of your car and into the house. Taking two trips seems like such a waste of time. So what do you do? You sling the backpack over a shoulder. You tuck the sweater under an armpit. You hold the keys in your teeth. You put the coffee on top of the car. You contort yourself every which way to get arms into the back seat, because the backpack doesn't allow you to duck fully inside the door. You groan, stretching whichever remaining fingers aren't already holding the phone, trying to loop bag handles.

Is it really saving you time over having made two darned trips?

And that's to say nothing of the host of catastrophes you're tempting fate to rain down upon you by way of ripped bags, broken eggs, spilled coffee (which of course splashes on the white sweater you were carrying), a phone drop that cracks the screen—or worse yet, a tweaked shoulder that lays you up for days.

So if this flavor of acting in haste doesn't tend to end well, why is it so prevalent as to have resulted in a warning that's lasted for centuries?

As I think about this, I'm able to identify perhaps five reasons we continue with haste despite the high risk of waste. I'll share them with you, along with a few thoughts on each.

1. Poor Planning

While it's not the main focus of our chapter, there's another well-worn saying that's worth introducing here:

"Failure to plan is planning to fail."

In *The Best Advice So Far*, I offer a different variation on the same theme:

**"Don't just *not plan* to get into trouble;
plan not to get into trouble."**

Consider that the many proverbs on the matter aren't persuasive doctrines that somehow *created* behaviors and consequences. They're merely observations—*descriptions* of patterns so universal as to be assumed to be *true*. In other words, a lasting piece of wisdom such as "haste makes waste" qualifies as *just plain common sense*. And yet if such sensibility is, indeed, common... why, as I say, do we need the reminder in the first place?

The answer to that question is twofold and as old as humanity itself: *emotion* and *egocentrism*. And both spring from the same well. That is, it is human nature to perceive that personal experience supersedes physical evidence; and that what applies to the general population does not apply the same way to me, because I am special.

And so, for instance, there's no denying that planning takes time. The "wing-it" approach then, as well as out-and-out procrastination, makes us *feel like* we're actually *gaining* time. And even if "haste makes waste" for those other people out there, it won't apply to me because I'm especially skilled and brilliant.

Of course, operating on unchecked personal experience and egocentrism despite proof to the contrary is also the definition of *delusional thinking*.

And so, as it turns out, the only smart and rational thing to do is check our feelings in favor of the facts and adjust accordingly.

That said, here are a few quick tips to help get you started toward better planning and less of the waste that comes with haste.

Plan the next day—at least the morning—the night before. Choose and set out clothes. Set out your toiletries, hair dryer, toothpaste and any other routine items you use to get ready. Pack tomorrow's lunch.

As simple as this advice is, *get enough sleep.* If you're a snooze-a-holic in the morning, set your waking alarm to something loud and annoying (no "gentle harp") and then keep it far enough away from you that you *have to* get out of bed to turn it off.

Start using the calendar and reminder apps on your mobile phone. Use the alert feature to give yourself a couple of notices ahead of time. I typically use "1 day" and "2 hours" in combination, with good success.

Plan planning time. Literally add "Planning" blocks to your calendar. High school teachers and college syllabuses broke down long-term assignments *for* us; but as adults, it's *our* responsibility to plan those milestones that lead to success on larger or more complex goals and tasks.

As you begin to solidify a better routine—one relatively free of haste and waste—post reminders to yourself somewhere you'll see them at key times. A sticky note with "Haste makes waste" attached to the bathroom mirror or a similar screensaver for your laptop can be that additional external voice you need in order to remember your new goal—until that voice is so deeply ingrained that it becomes your own.

2. People Pleasing

Dating and marriage aren't the only relationships people jump into. Saying *yes* when others ask for our help or participation or money, with no further consideration than whether or not they'll like us if we don't, is *still* a form of haste. And this can leave us routinely exhausted, swindled—even feeling bitter or bullied. This form of hasty decision-making is a waste of our personal (and limited, I might add) resources of energy, time and money.

I used to say *yes* to just about everything in my younger years. There's a whole chapter on how I kicked my addiction to *yes* in *The Best Advice So Far*. But here, I'll offer just a couple of brief tips for those who know what I'm talking about.

I used to think that **yes** was nice and **no** was mean. I then moved to thinking that **no** was necessary. But **no** can actually be the nicest thing you say to someone.

By way of example, let me take the *other person's* perspective for a bit here: that of the *person asking* something, rather than the *yes*-man.

I love to collaborate with creative people. Creating by myself is terrific. But there are just some forms of creative venture that feel better and go further when you have other people involved who are equally invested and capable. They bring their own perspective and skills to a project, which can elevate it and take it in a direction that you yourself may never have stumbled upon.

I say I love to collaborate. But the truth is, I don't do it often.

Now, I *try* to do it fairly often. I will get talking with

someone and the topic of our shared creative passion will come up. Somewhere along the line in that conversation, my wheels begin to turn in a new direction and I start seeing the possibilities that this meeting of the minds could have if jointly applied. So I'll say, "Hey, would you like to collaborate on something together? I could do this and you could do that, and we could really come up with something great! What do you think?"

This is most often met with an enthusiastic (and hasty) *"YES! Great! Let's do it!"*

Being me, I can't sleep. I'm too excited. So I get right to work, burning the midnight oil, pouring myself out into my part of the collaboration. I don't want to hold things back!

Soon, I have something—something that feels strong and alive. I present it to my new collaboration partner, and they exclaim its virtues and promise (again, hastily) to get to work on their part in it.

A week passes. Then two. Then a month. No word.

I'll check in and see if there is anything else I can do. Are they getting anywhere? Would it be better to meet up in person and work together? Are they feeling inspired by the part I offered, or would they rather trash it and start things off themselves?

Here, explanations for the delay are proffered. Promises are made. But communication wanes and enthusiasm fizzles.

It can get a guy down, I tell you.

Let's go back to that first meeting, when the idea of a collaboration was introduced. The *"YES!"* from the other person *felt* "nice" at the time. But at the end of the day, was it *really nice*?

If you, like me, struggle with saying **no**, consider that by politely declining, you may actually be doing the **nicest** thing.

Your **no** allows the other person to have realistic expectations.

Your **no** allows them to continue their pursuit for someone else who may be a legitimate **yes**, rather than merely waiting and hoping and wasting time.

Your **no** allows communication between the two of you to continue unencumbered, without the awkwardness or avoidance that comes with having said **yes** when you really meant **no**.

No is not mean.

No is not even merely necessary.

No is nice.

"But," you protest, "I *never* bail on people! I always follow through on the things I commit to doing." Please know, I'm with you. I can honestly say that I've never missed a deadline for something I said I'd do. I give my very best.

And that's part of the problem.

Every block of time during which I give my all to something else… is a block of time I *take away from myself and my own pursuits.* Conversely, every time you say *no,* you are saying *yes* to something else—perhaps something more important or worthwhile.

I'm not suggesting that generously giving of our time, money or talents to others is a bad thing. I still do it more often than most. I'm merely saying *don't operate in haste.* Take time to consider what you're getting yourself into— and what else you might be choosing to say *no* to with that *yes* you are about to utter.

Let me suggest a valuable tool, one I use so consistently at this point that most people I know have come to accept it as par for the course when asking for my involvement in just about anything.

I call it my "Three-Day Rule."

My Three-Day Rule goes into effect any time I'm asked to take on something new that will require more than an hour of my time.

This applies to energy expenditure as well. Most people don't have a very good understanding of the energy and time that careful thought and planning require. For instance, while I may be asked to speak or to lead a workshop for a single hour of in-person time, the thought and planning that I'll put into the *creation* of that one hour might be *20 or 30* hours.

Let's look at a case in point. Suppose Joe asks me if I could help him edit a book he's written. First—and this is a valuable skill in itself, one that took me many years to figure out—if editing Joe's book is something I have absolutely no desire, time or energy to do, I simply say, "I won't be able to help you with that, Joe." No need for apologies or further explanation. (See Chapter 29 of *The Best Advice So Far*: "Saying No").

On the other hand, if it's something I might consider, I bring out my Three-Day Rule. I smile and reply with "Give me three days to consider it and get back to you." Even if my initial reaction to helping Joe edit his book is an enthusiastic one, I don't jump to saying *yes*. I've come to realize that the good will of a moment can absolutely ruin weeks or months afterward without allowing myself time for careful consideration first.

At this point, Joe may try to press me into an immediate answer. "Well, I was really hoping to have it all edited by this weekend," he says. My next reply will be, "I've come to trust and rely on my Three-Day Rule, Joe; so if you need it edited right away, I'm not your guy. Good luck." (Remember from the previous discussion here that *saying no is nice*: nice to Joe, by way of setting realistic expectations he can plan around—and nice to *yourself*.)

On the other hand, Joe might say, "OK, that'd be great, thanks." In this case, I set a reminder in my phone to get back to Joe in three days, along with two alerts beforehand to remind me to be thinking about it. And then *I really do think about it*. And I get back to Joe with a *yes* or a *no* on the day I said I would.

If Joe texts me after one day and says, "Any thoughts on helping me edit?"… I reply, "Still need my three days. ☺"

Keep in mind that the focus here isn't whether or not you help edit a book. This is a broad principle, one meant to keep you from overloading yourself so that *haste*—and the resulting *waste*—are increasingly eliminated from your life. If I'd applied my Three-Day Rule before jumping into that wretched editor position I mentioned at the start of this chapter, I'd most certainly have had plenty of time to see the pitfalls of the situation with clarity and thus avoided six months of misery.

Let me add a couple more quick thoughts here regarding the Three-Day Rule, in case you're thinking about adopting it yourself.

First, wherever possible, start by giving the requester

some specific responsibility. For instance, with Joe and his book-editing request, I might say, "Send me an email with the total word count, a synopsis and a clear description of the types of edits you'd like me to consider making; *then give me three days to consider.*" You'd be surprised at the percentage of would-be requests that'll be weeded out entirely by prefacing your Three-Day Rule with even the most basic prerequisites.

By the way, the Three-Day Rule doesn't just apply to requests made of you.

Imagine your co-worker Jack tells you he's overheard Veronica spreading lies about you at the office. Or an ex sends you a hateful text (or another "let's-get-back-together" text). Or you read a particularly virulent, misleading and flat-out erroneous political post on social media. You know full well what you *want* to do (because, let's be honest, it's what you *typically* do). If you're like me, what you *want* to do is respond posthaste, setting records straight and letting those emotions (and, of course, your superior intellect) fly. You want this problem solved. And you want it solved *right now*.

I can only assure you from experience that you'll save yourself much drama and woe (i.e., more **waste** of time and energy) if you'll apply the Three-Day Rule without fail before responding to *anyone* or *anything* where you recognize that your emotions are riled. Often times, in so doing, problems solve themselves in the meantime. Veronica gets transferred. The ex sends another text saying, "I was drunk. Never mind." Somebody else sets the social media post straight, or the original poster deletes it. And for those times when the issue still exists after three days, you'll be much more likely to address it with grace, logic and a level head than if you'd indulged in haste.

3. Efficiency

Despite our experience with mishaps, many of us continue to want to believe that hurrying is the same as being efficient. And we see efficiency as either a virtue or a necessity. But take a quick look at a widely accepted definition of the word:

> **efficiency** | *the ability to avoid wasting materials, energy, efforts, money, and time in doing something or in producing a desired result*

Considering the fairly typical example of the grocery bag fiasco I mentioned earlier, it's clear that the waste could easily evidence itself in *every facet* of an attempt at efficiency: materials, energy, efforts, money and time. Playing that out, let's say you were to *succeed* in saving a minute and have no mishaps nine out of ten times you tried to fit two car-to-house trips into one (you won't, but let's suppose). A ruined item or an injury—even just *one time* out of ten—would result in losses that far exceed the nine minutes saved during prior "successful haste." Replacing a phone screen or paying to get coffee stains out of a sweater costs you *real money*, not to mention the hours of time you'll now need to set aside to go to the store or dry cleaners. A shot shoulder or neck, and you'll waste effort through pain and loss of mobility, not to mention more money in time out of work.

In other words, if waste is the one thing that must be avoided in order to achieve efficiency, and haste *makes* waste…

Yup. The logical conclusion is that haste is actually *antithetical* to efficiency.

4. Impatience

For some, the issue isn't being pressed for time. It's a sheer lack of patience. This leads the dog to chase its tail where haste is concerned. That is, impatience leads to haste; haste leads to waste; and waste leads to more impatience.

Patience isn't fostered in a digital age. To the contrary, it's trained right out of us, to the point where waiting—for anything, really—causes us to become not only uncomfortable but downright indignant.

If there's a holdup at the drive-through, we suck our teeth and chirp our tires as we swerve out of line, glaring in the direction of the sliding window on our way past. But what do we do then? We think to ourselves, "I'll show *you*. I'll drive right over to your *competitor* and give *them* my money"—never stopping long enough to consider that this hasty decision will in all likelihood require *more* time than if we'd waited a few minutes more before throwing our consumeristic tantrum.

One short passage from *The Best Advice So Far* bears repeating here:

> *Patience, by definition, is the ability to graciously wait. It stands to reason, then, that if I no longer have to wait, I will no*

longer have opportunities to build patience.
And that leaves me being impatient.

Impatient with stoplights that aren't
turning when I will them to.

Impatient with learning a new skill or
sticking with a new undertaking.

Impatient when others do not get out
what they are saying fast enough for my
liking.

Impatient with the natural foibles and
learning curves of my children.

As patience wanes, other things expand
to fill the void. Stress. Irritation. Head-
aches. High blood pressure. Anger.

The waste we create in the haste of our impatience, then, extends beyond the moment. The more we indulge it, the more it accumulates, making a rubbish pile of our peace, our happiness—and our relationships.

5. Habit

Where the pursuit of ever-increasing efficiency meets the impatience borne of technology, habit is born. And in all fairness, this habit of haste isn't always a self-inflicted one. In a quest for ever more "efficiency and productivity," employers push workers to the point where eight hours of hard work is no longer enough.

My best friend worked in regional sales for several years. At the end of each quarter, the "big bosses" would post for all to see the roster of who met or fell short of their quotas and by how much—all ranked from "sales stars"…

to bottom feeders. This public listing was purportedly done in order to recognize top sellers. But make no mistake: the primary purpose was public shaming.

Well, as it so happens, my friend was *great* at what she did. Her customers loved her, and she met her sales goals every time. So she was always a star, never a bottom feeder. *C'est la vie.* However… she quickly realized the trap that was set, even for those at the top. First, "The List" created an environment of negativity. Those who weren't in the "star" category were perpetually frustrated, envious, even spiteful of those who *were*. And no matter *how* much revenue you generated, you got your five minutes at the top of "The List"—which became oddly programmed to mean something—and then your *new* quota for the next quarter was increased by another 5%. *Ad infinitum.*

Before long, she was routinely driving 50 miles north to see two clients, then driving 75 miles south for another, 50 more miles west for yet another (who'd forget she was scheduled to come), only to drive 75 miles back to where she'd just been to see another client who wanted a later appointment—all while surreptitiously checking her watch and feeling her heart beating in her throat. She badly injured her shoulder, yanking and pushing trunks of merchandise breathlessly into and out of her vehicle; but there was no slowing down even for that if she were going to meet the new sales goals. Nine-hour days turned into 10- and 12-hour days or longer. She stopped gardening. Stopped baking. Stopped reading. Home-cooked meals were replaced with take-out. In short, she was a very tired and unhappy "star."

From teachers to techies, physicians to fishermen, we

become conditioned, like Pavlov's dogs, to run at full tilt at all times—*even* during those rare times when there's no actual reason for it. This is why after a semester ends, or we've traded our briefcase for beach sandals, it can take days or even longer for our brains to kick into "vacation mode." Taking things slow feels somehow *wrong*; and ironically, a leisurely pace can induce restlessness, distractibility, insomnia, guilt and a host of other negative effects.

And so we keep running.

But the waste that results isn't just a spilled coffee or a shattered mug. These things of some little value can be replaced. There are far greater "wastes" we create.

I recently came across a quote attributed to music and film legend Doris Day:

"I love to laugh. It's the only way to live.
Enjoy each day—it's not coming back again."

As my best friend would say, "Boy, isn't *that* the truth!" I'm happy to report that she made good use of that all-important power of *choice*. She left that position for one where she is valued as more than a money machine—and where she once again has *time* for the important things.

You see, the truly *tragic* waste that results from allowing ourselves to remain in a perpetual state of busyness—is the waste of *time*, which cannot for all the money in the world be regained. If we're always waiting for that two-week vacation before we allow ourselves to relax, not only will we be sorely disappointed as our habitual haste eats up most of that time off, we waste—day by day, week by week, year by year—the *one* lifetime we are given.

Furthermore, habitual haste leaves no time for reflection, and this dooms us to repeat the same mistakes over and over again.

But it gets worse still. A perpetual state of hurrying doesn't merely affect ourselves. If we don't make time to slow down—to truly connect with the people around us—we also waste *relationships*. Like an untended garden, these too wither and die without patient care and nurturing. Spouses drift apart. Grown children move out and move on, seldom visiting. No friends come calling anymore.

If you hear nothing else, hear this: *the haste of today is the waste of tomorrow.*

Not TRUE

"Haste makes waste" is a unidirectional piece of wisdom. That is, while haste often causes waste, *not* all waste is the result of haste.

You may be an extraordinarily skilled basketball player who practices diligently and daily—and you'll still lose games.

You've spent years writing and editing that novel, or tweaking songs for that album, only to be discouraged by meager sales.

Perhaps you launched a start-up after months of hard work and preparation, and based on an idea that market research showed was a sure winner—only to wind up shuttering the doors after six quarters.

Maybe you've even struggled for years sincerely trying to save your marriage, yet you still got gut punched when the divorce papers were handed to you.

And I don't care how careful you might be in your workouts, you *still* may wind up throwing your back out.

Robert Burns poignantly expressed this in his 1785 poem entitled "To a Mouse," which was written in Scots. Here's an apropos excerpt:

> **But Mousie, thou art no thy-lane,**
> **In proving foresight may be vain:**
> **The best laid schemes o' Mice an' Men**
> **Gang aft agley,**
> **An' lea'e us nought but grief an' pain,**
> **For promis'd joy!**

Many of you will have recognized another old gem of wisdom in there, though you're most likely familiar with the more modern translation:

> **The best laid plans of mice and men**
> **often go awry.**

So the other team simply outplayed you this time based on excellence and dedication that rival your own. Or you're a great producer, but not a marketing expert. As my best friend's mom put it many years ago, "The sooner you realize that life is not fair, the happier you will be." Sometimes accidents, mishaps, losses and failures just *happen*. There is no blame to be placed. And in such cases, true success or failure is measured by what you choose to do *next*.

Also note that there is a difference between haste and

mere *speed*. John Heywood made this distinction clear when he placed the two in counterpoint: *"The more haste, the less speed."* Quality experts worldwide will tell you that the kind of efficiency they are paid to develop and implement is designed around finding the path of least wasted effort *without error*. And there is a certain amount of speed necessarily involved in achieving that aim.

However, tying speed, efficiency and "the best laid plans" together, I want to note that it is possible to be *fast and efficient*—absent of haste—and still have waste or error occur. Allow me to give one amusing anecdote that I trust will make this point both clear and memorable.

Among other things, I'm a pianist. I've played since I was three years old. One of my crowning achievements in junior high school was having been able to play Rachmaninoff's *Prelude in C# Minor*. If you don't know the piece, you'll get more out of this story (and some good old-fashioned entertainment besides) by giving it a listen. While the piece starts off almost laboriously slow and somber, it crescendos and intensifies as it progresses to the point of near impossible fury. So there I was as a teenager, playing the piece in concert, having wound to the top of the roller coaster ready to take the audience plummeting with me... when the high-B string on the piano snapped, whipped forward with a crack, and sliced the right side of my face about an inch from my eye. Still, with the slack string now buzzing as it lay across others, a dead high B, and blood now streaming down my face from a stinging gash, I'll have you know I finished that piece with aplomb (not to mention flair and drama).

I played it nearly flawlessly, a piece that played as

intended most definitely requires *speed*. Yet error was introduced nonetheless. Imperfection. "Waste," if you will, of an otherwise perfect moment. Why? Well, because for us mice and men and everyone in between, we still live in an imperfect world where the best laid plans go awry. I'm famous for saying in these situations, "It's just another party story waiting to happen." And see, even now, here I am captivating readers with this thrilling tale (*grin*)— all because of what went "*wrong*."

Just as speed is not synonymous with haste, "quick thinking" and "decisive action" are not necessarily the same as making hasty decisions. I had to think quick and take decisive action, for instance, when that piano string let go. Haste, in the context of Heywood's warning, is defined as "*excessive* speed or urgency," not merely "speed or urgency." So when your child is running obliviously toward the road chasing that shiny red ball of theirs, that's *not* the time for circumspection. You drop what you're doing (even if literally), you bolt, and you grab that child by any means necessary. Similarly, we count on surgeons to be able to make split-second decisions during an operation. Sometimes, an immediate response is required.

In similar vein, a *timely* response is often called for. One should not use "haste makes waste" as a handy excuse to indefinitely sit on fences. By all means, where possible, take time for careful consideration. But there is a world of difference between a Three-Day Rule and a Three-Month *Ruse*. Don't hold up other people's plans, progress—or *lives*—under the guise of wisdom. This brings to mind a more modern if crass saying involving timely action, a potty word and, well... a *pot*. I trust you catch my drift.

While we're fine tuning the notion of what does and does not constitute haste, note the delineation between procrastination and planned delay. The former may leave us cornered into forced haste, and thus waste, down the road. The quintessential example would be *avoiding* study or a work project until just before the deadline. This often results in a subpar end result (i.e., the waste of potential). Even if you're able to pull off a credible job at the last minute, honest self-assessment may show that you traded (i.e., wasted) *peace of mind* in the process. By contrast, planned delay is based on accurate self-awareness and does *not* replace peace of mind with panic. Some people just work *best* closer to deadline than if they were to start too far in advance.

I know this because I'm one of those people.

I recollect my thesis supervisor admonishing me and my peers: "This is a semester-long project. And be fore-warned that if your thesis paper is less than a bare mini-mum of 50 pages, I can guarantee that you haven't covered all of the existing research. And that means I will have no choice but to reject your work."

Professor Anderson was one of my favorite professors. I respected her greatly. But I knew myself. If I started that thesis when she suggested, it would have been lackluster. There's a certain amount of urgency that's needed to set my creativity ablaze. What's more, I chose a topic that really *was* new ground at the time, and thus there was strikingly little previous research in the journals.

Professor Anderson checked in with me before Christmas break, the final thesis being due when we returned in January. I told her that the research on my narrow topic was scant and that I hadn't yet started the paper, but assured her that there was no need for worry. Her look was 90% incredulity, 8% curiosity and 2% amusement (yes, exactly). Once she composed herself, she took a deep breath and said simply, "I trust you."

I wrote the entire thing in the last 48 hours of the break.

When I handed it over to Professor Anderson and she felt the slight heft, she nibbled her bottom lip and flipped to the last sheet. Nineteen pages. Her expression was about the same, I imagine, as a parent whose son has just told her in the last year of medical school that he's decided he really wants to be a stage magician instead. She shook her head, though one corner of her lips had quirked upward, not unkindly. "Erik," she said, "if anyone could have pulled this off, it's you. I'm happy to be proven wrong here."

A few weeks later, she gathered everyone in my group and silently handed back our papers. I saw a few faces turn white. Or red. When mine was the only one remaining, she walked gravely toward me and stopped, the paper held tightly to her chest. Then she turned it over with a wink and the slightest of smiles.

Highest marks.

My best friend, whom I mentioned earlier, knows this about me—that I perform best under pressure. She and I have worked together on countless projects that would take many people weeks or months to plan and prepare for, and yet she's always saying to me, "I'm sure you'll be writing your talk out on the steering wheel on the way there—and it will be great."

There's no particular benefit or edge to planning things close to the wire, as opposed to taking the slow-and-steady approach. I merely felt it necessary to point out, for the sake of some readers who may identify with this trait, that eleventh-hour planning isn't *necessarily* haste. Again, for me, planning too far *in advance* would be the waste, costing a project in terms of creativity, inspiration and finesse. For others, planning well ahead of time is *crucial*, and waiting until the last minute would be disastrous. It all goes back to the challenge presented in Chapter 1: "Know thyself."

"Haste makes waste" should also not be interpreted as a call to eliminate spontaneity from your life altogether. Yes, perhaps that tipsy trek to a Vegas wedding chapel is the kind of spontaneity that's best avoided. But rigid routine, fear of change, or just plain being a stick-in-the-mud is guaranteed to waste more *life* than most of the possible hazards that may accompany haste.

After my father divorced my mother, I watched a rock of a woman erode before my very eyes. My mother had been a bastion of responsibility in every regard her entire life, and what it seemed to have gotten her after thirty years of marriage was despair. She soldiered through her night shifts as a nursing supervisor. She went to church and left. She drove the same routes. She ate the same tasteless meals. Day after day. Her skin was waxy and pale, her eyes always moist, her nose perpetually red. She was clinging to routine. But that routine was also pinning her to an ever deepening depression that *included thinking the same thoughts*, over and over and over again.

One day in the endless murk, she attended a staff training on the power of laughter in healing. In the state she found herself, it was sandpaper against an open wound. She shared with me how she'd instantly labeled the speaker as a "new-age quack." After it was over (which couldn't have been soon enough as far as she was concerned), she drove her same old route home, retracing the steps of the heartache and unfairness of her life. Then, stopped at a notoriously long traffic light, she happened to glance over at the passenger seat where she'd tossed the documentation from the training. Atop it was a red foam clown nose, which had been included as some sort of memory token of the day's talk. I don't know why she did it, but my miserable mother reached over, picked up that clown nose and popped it on over her own already red nose.

Now, some of you may be thinking, "That's a nice story. But what the heck does it have to do with haste?" Let me reiterate that "haste," for some, has come to mean acting impulsively, emotionally, irrationally or "without a darned good reason." My point here is that *sometimes*, the very best thing we can do when we're in a hard rut is to follow those fleeting thoughts that tell us there is something beyond the drudgery of the cycle we're in. Joy, surprise, curiosity—all of these are experienced spur of the moment, what some might call "whims." But that's not haste. That's *living*.

So there was my mom at the red light, wearing her foam clown nose on a somber face. She looked to her left, just as the man in the vehicle beside her also happened to turn his head her way.

The windows between them became the screen of a silent movie as the man threw his head back and laughed. And that laughter cut through the clouds like a ray of sunlight. Despite herself, my mother began to giggle as well—which only made the two of them laugh all the harder.

The light turned green and these two strangers who had shared a moment of spontaneous laughter together continued on their ways. But my mom's way was now *different*.

She kept that clown nose right in her armrest compartment and used it often thereafter. In fact, she put it on at the climax of telling me that story, and we had another laugh in the kitchen.

Remember that haste involves *excessive* speed or lack of consideration before action. The key to spontaneity is to match the amount of consideration to the potential consequence. Often, this can be done in a minute or two rather than hours or days. The negative repercussions of donning a clown nose in traffic, for example, are pretty minimal by any measure. And so even an ultra-responsible person like my mom could make that small, even silly, choice in an instant.

All that is to say that leaving the dirty dishes until tomorrow in favor of an impromptu drive to the beach one night might be just the thing. In fact, you may find that the dishes get done twice as fast when you return.

The cure for haste, as with most things, comes down to *present choice*—even if that simple choice in this moment is to slow down, take a pause for some honest reflection and make just one lasting change.

Questions & A Challenge

1. Many forms and causes of haste were discussed in this chapter, along with the types of waste they can cause. Which do you most identify with? Can you recall a clear example of a time when haste caused waste for you?

2. How difficult do you think it would be to adopt the "Three-Day Rule"? What are some specific areas in which a "rule" like this might help you avoid hastily saying yes to people and situations?

3. Is there a relationship in your life that you may be wasting to some degree as a result of busyness (a form of haste)? What is one measure you could take to bring things back into balance with that person?

CHALLENGE: This quote from the chapter bears repeating: "*...sometimes, the very best thing we can do when we're in a hard rut is to follow those fleeting thoughts that tell us there is something beyond the drudgery of the cycle we're in. Joy, surprise, curiosity—all of these are experienced spur of the moment, what some might call 'whims.' But that's not haste. That's living.*" A great way to incorporate spontaneity into your day is to allow yourself to follow your natural curiosity— to find out more about something that pops into your awareness. Make a conscious decision to break from routine at some point during the next three days and to do something spontaneous. By nature, you can't plan spontaneity; but you can plan *for* it. Perhaps set a couple phone reminders that simply say, "Are you allowing yourself to be spontaneous?" Once you've met that part of the challenge, tell a friend about your experience.

7

stitch

IN THE LAST CHAPTER we spent a good while digging into the history and wisdom behind "Haste makes waste." I trust you're now standing on solid footing with all of that; because I'm about to suggest that, sometimes, it's not haste but *waiting* that makes waste.

I once had a roommate whom I'll call "Seamus" here, for the sake of protecting the guilty. Every roommate I'd had prior to Seamus had been a friend I already knew. But when the then-current roommate left me in the lurch by breaking the lease to move in with his girlfriend, I was forced for the first time to put out an ad and brace myself to invite a stranger in.

There wasn't time to be overly picky, so I settled on a guy who worked locally and whose short response to my ad read thusly:

Clean, quiet, respectful male.
Mid-thirties. Employed.

What I wound up with instead was a teenager disguised in the body of a man, one who returned from work each night with a twelve-pack of "Natty Ice," retired to his dark room, sat in his ratty recliner, and played video games until three in the morning on full volume. The shooting, crashing and screaming from the giant speakers was interrupted occasionally by loud bouts of swearing or drawn-out burping.

And he was not, by any stretch of the imagination, *clean*.

It was a nightmare. I honestly don't know how a neatnik like me survived it. The tales I could tell would make your toes curl and your blood curdle, from disturbing bathroom habits, to bringing home a drunk hookup whose name he did not know and who made a habit of peeing on my furniture in the… shall we say "wee" hours.

There was the night I woke up needing some ibuprofen, felt my way into the dim kitchen, then slipped and landed in—and I'm not exaggerating—a gallon or more of stinking sludge that was oozing across the floor. *What the…?*

The kitchen had been enemy territory for some time. I had given up all use of the stove shortly after Seamus moved in, as I'd quickly become overwhelmed trying to keep it clean. Not long before the oil slick, every resident in our building had been sent fleeing out into a subzero February morning at 2:00 AM, after Seamus had started boiling chicken on the range—then passed out drunk, leaving the contents of the pan as well as the growing mound of surrounding food scraps to catch fire and set the cabinets and entire back wall ablaze.

If only that had been the end of it, a lesson learned. *Au contraire*. You see, Seamus also saw no problem with routinely broiling various and sundry meats *directly on the oven rack*. No baking sheet. Not even tin foil underneath. It was this last penchant of his, as I was to discover, that was responsible for the creeping pool of goo that had nearly caused me to break my neck. The *entire lower drawer* of the stove was an effluvium of putrefying blood and grease, full to the brim and now finally overflowing onto the floor.

With the lights now on, I also noticed that, trapped in the only corner not yet overtaken by the encroaching gloop, were two critters who'd been rousted from their apparent home beneath the stove: a skittering centipede and a hairy black spider whose sizes suggest they had survived since the Cretaceous Period.

Try to imagine, if you will, how one even goes about trying to empty something like that oven drawer or to address the aftermath. To this day, I myself don't know, since I used a dishtowel to clean myself off as best I could, hopped to the dining area, marched in and woke Seamus on the spot, motioned that he should follow me, and pointed mutely at the open oven drawer and disaster zone of a kitchen—then took a shower and headed right back to bed.

I never did get that ibuprofen. And every last one of my baking dishes, cookie sheets and muffin tins had to be thrown away.

You're cringing. But alas… I haven't even gotten to the worst of it yet.

I woke one morning that summer, after Seamus had left for work, emerged from my room and headed to get my morning vitamins. En route, something thumped against my cheek—small, but sizable enough to startle me. I stopped to survey. *What had it been?* Turning left, I noticed two large, black flies bumbling against the windows. I meandered over, opened one of the windows and brushed the flies downward until they were trapped between the glass and the screen. *Slam.*

Meanwhile, my brain was churning. Having been struck on the right cheek, that could only mean that one of them had brushed by me on its way from—you guessed it—the

Kitchen of Doom. I sighed and braced myself for what I'd find when I turned the corner.

To my surprise, there was no especially foul odor. The kitchen wasn't *clean* by any means, mind you, and didn't smell of peaches and cream; but there was also no obvious source for flies that I could see. I tipped the trash bucket to take a look inside. Nothing. *Aha*, I thought, *he got up and found the trash crawling with flies. At least he was smart enough to empty it before I caught sight of it.*

Opening the cupboard to get a glass, I noticed that there was not a single plate—large or small—left on the shelves. I owned about 20. None in the sink, either; just a few greasy carving knives and splashes of condiments. I pulled the silverware drawer open. A couple spoons, no forks or steak knives. I closed my eyes and groaned audibly.

I plodded back up the short hall toward Seamus' room. A step or two from destination, I was greeted by the loud, rattling drone of an old air conditioner. Thing was... Seamus didn't *own* an air conditioner.

Another fly hit me, this time in the forehead. I looked down just as yet another fly wriggled its way from underneath Seamus' door, crawled upward an inch or so, and then whizzed by me toward the living room.

Warily, I turned the doorknob.

Without even stepping inside, the stench that emanated from the mere crack I'd opened the door was enough to gag me. But it was the *sound* that set my skin to crawling. Holding my breath, I scanned the cave with widened eyes. That's when I beheld the source of the strident buzzing...

Hundreds upon hundreds of carrion flies blotted out the sunlight as they frantically crawled up the window panes and over one another in their frenzied struggle to escape.

Barely visible in the murk, silhouetted against the writhing backdrop, were all of my plates and silverware, stacked in two precarious towers that rose up from a rickety TV tray—gristle, bone and gelatinized blood glistening moistly between the spaces. The heat and thick humidity of August had made the macabre assemblage the perfect breeding ground for a horde of maggots, all of which had apparently had time to pupate and then hatch on this fateful day.

TRIED

A stitch in time saves nine.

You may recall from Chapter 5 an Englishman by the name of Thomas Fuller. If not, don't fret; you're not slipping. By way of reminder, his work (*The History of The Worthies of England* served as a brief way station on our quest to follow the written trail that eventually led to "A penny saved is a penny earned." Here, however, Thomas Fuller will have his moment to shine.

You'll also likely remember from Chapter 6 the comically long title of one of John Heywood's collections. I can only surmise that verbose book titles were in vogue at the time, as Fuller seems determined to have given Heywood a run for his money with this beauty:

Gnomologia: Adagies and Proverbs, Wise Sentences and Witty Sayings, Ancient and Modern, Foreign and British

And it's this grandly-titled work of Fuller's that brings us this chapter's proverb: "A stitch in time saves nine."

I admit, before I even sunk my teeth into the proverb itself, I couldn't help but indulge my curiosity about this volume.

First, I was sure that "Adagies" was a misspelling. Turns out it isn't. And now that I know this, it does sound rather quaint, doesn't it?

Then there was the leading word of that title: *Gnomologia*. I thought, *What could little dwarfish garden folk possibly have to do with such a book*? (And don't shake your head at me; you know you were thinking the same thing.) Turns out, there are *two* disparate definitions for the English word "gnome," each of which hails from different origins. The Latin *gnomus* referred to a mythical race of tiny people, giving way to the concept of our present-day garden gnomes. The entirely unrelated Greek word *gnōmē*, however, simply translated as "thought" or "opinion" and came to mean any short saying intended to teach a lesson or moral.

I, for one, feel smarter for knowing this.

Let's set aside the peculiar title and move on to talking a bit more about the writer. If you were to look up "Thomas Fuller" and read only the first line of the first entry, you'd likely read something like this: "Thomas Fuller (1608—1661) was an English churchman and historian." But when he was born and died, and even what he wrote, isn't who Thomas Fuller *was*. As helpful as such entries are in many ways, they do make it all too easy to forget that these historical "figures" were *real people*, living *real lives* not so unlike yours and mine. As a writer myself, it's of particular interest to know, for instance, that Fuller was one of the first early English writers to be able to earn a living entirely off of his writing. After a bit of digging, I was pleased to have also uncovered this beautifully *human* description of Fuller, written by a friend:

> *His unfailing playfulness, the exuberant wit, often extravagant, rarely ineffective and always unforced, is combined with a kindliness and simplicity which never fails to charm. If not profound, he is invariably shrewd, sound-hearted, and sensible. He tells a story admirably... with infectious enjoyment. His humour is childlike in its freedom from bitterness. His quick sense of the ridiculous, combined with a calm and cheerful temperament, made fanaticism impossible.*

For me, this personal description *does* lend a fresh perspective to the title. Was Fuller being intentionally "extravagant" and "ridiculous" in stringing so many words together, or even in choosing the odd word "Gnomologia"? I rather think this may be the case, as I get a clear taste of Fuller's wit and "humour" in some of the opening notes from the book:

> *Adagies and proverbs are to be accounted only as sauce to relish meat with, but not as substantial dishes to make a meal on; and therefore are never good, but upon proper*

> *subjects and occasions, where they may*
> *serve to give a lively force and pleasant*
> *turn to whatever is said; but to apply them*
> *wrong or crack them off too thick, like*
> *Sancha* [sic] *in* Don Quixote, *is abominably*
> *foppish, ridiculous, and nauseous.*

Tell us how you *really* feel, Thomas.

Yet I'm inclined to agree with him. As is the case when people attempt to throw in advanced vocabulary, political opinions, religious quotes or moral platitudes without really knowing what the heck they're talking about, slinging a great proverb out of context or used incorrectly serves neither listener nor speaker well. Therein lay the impetus for my having written the book you're now reading.

Like me, Fuller made no pretense of having invented the wisdom he gathered (though, apparently, he *did* include a smattering of his own observations and sayings as well). Likewise, for Fuller, as for most authors including myself, his book was a passion project written solely for the benefit of an audience of people he envisioned only in his heart and mind, knowing that he'd likely never meet those readers.

It's also fairly evident from his front material that Fuller had to deal with his share of naysayers who rolled their eyes and wagged their tongues at his life's work, thinking it a waste of time or too pedestrian and easily consumable for "real thinkers" to pay it any mind:

> *And having at length collected more than*
> *ever any Englishman has before me, I have*
> *ventur'd to send them forth, to try their*

fortune among the people... It's a matter of no small pains and diligence (whatever lazy, snarling persons may think) to pick up so many independent particulars, as I have here done... These things being undeniably so, no man ought despise, ridicule, or in any ways discourage the diligence and kindness of those, that take pains to bring home to others... those things of profit and pleasure.

Anyone who's ever written anything and tried to have it published, or who has held out any personal creative work for public consumption (and often, therefore, criticism) has at some time or other experienced similar feelings. This makes it all the more piteous to know that Fuller pushed through the hard work and negativity to complete his labor of love, yet would never in his lifetime see it "[brought] home to others." In fact, it wasn't until 1732—more than 70 years after Fuller's death—that the book would finally be published, leaving *others* to collect royalties on a valuable book they themselves didn't toil over.

Now that you've got a more intimate understanding of the man who penned the words, what of the proverb itself: "A stitch in time saves nine"?

First, the adage predates Fuller; for by the time he felt it worthy of inclusion, it was *already* considered an established saying. As with so many other valuable pieces of wisdom passed down from yore, exactly how old it is may never be known. What we do know, however, is that we have Thomas Fuller to thank for its having survived to our day.

As to meaning, those unfamiliar with the saying may at first wonder whether "a stitch in time" indicates some uncanny ancient understanding of astrophysics. That would've been cool. But no—this is no reference to the rending or repair of the space-time continuum.

This inclusion in Fuller's collection—in keeping with his own description as having been simple, sound-hearted and sensible—is fairly straightforward once we know the context: *mending clothes*. Paraphrased into prose, the axiom might read something like this: "If you sew the tear in a sock the moment you notice it, you'll use just one stitch and minimal effort. Put it off, however, and that tear will get exponentially worse, until it requires a good many more stitches to fix."

This seems an excellent time to pause and truly appreciate the genius of a well-stated proverb: its ability to convey so much in so few words.

Of course, anymore, if our sock or pant crotch or shirt sleeve were to snag and tear, we'd just throw it out and buy another. And so it will take some backward-reaching empathy to understand that this was not the way of things for most of the human timeline. Processed cloth was not easy to come by, even for the wealthy, and all the more rare for the commoner. And the cleaning process was much harsher than we enjoy thanks to our washing machines with easy-care cycles and such. So it was just a routine chore to collect household clothing, inspect each article for damage and then "darn" any items in need of repair.

The wise knew that leaving a small tear unattended, while allowing some small leisure in the present moment, would leave *future-you* with ten times the work. And that seemed an obviously terrible trade-off. What's more, in a day when the average family would only have been able to afford for each member to own a single pair of trousers, or one "sensible dress" and one for Sundays, a runaway rip could very well mean the end of an essential garment that might have reasonably lasted years longer given timely care. Let a sock tear through, and you may have been forced to wrap a foot in strips of burlap—or nothing at all—during the cold, wet months until you might at last be able to replace it.

...&...

A couple of chapters back, I provided some trivia about how I came by the cover illustration for this book. Here, I'll offer another little morsel. It was "A stitch in time saves nine" that put the notion in my head to write *Tried & (Still) True* in the first place. I'd had a growing awareness of just how much useful language was being lost with each new decade. I'd even had several discussions with friends about it. But then I overheard a snippet of a public exchange between an older woman and her teenage grandson. She raised her eyebrows, intending to gently chide him: "A stitch in time…"

There was an awkward pause as the young man stared at her like she was suddenly speaking Turkish. A few beats later, he offered a noncommittal "Uhhh…" after which he simply shook his head in bewilderment, and the subject was dropped.

I had no idea what the nature of their discussion had

been, nor whether the older woman had been justified in her use of the partial proverb. What *was* clear, however, was that there was a complete generational disconnect—that the teen had absolutely no idea what his elder was talking about.

And it struck me in that moment how sad it was that centuries, even millennia, worth of concise wisdom was dying out. I wondered aloud, "Would *anyone* under the age of thirty recognize it anymore if they were to hear 'a stitch in time'?" So I determined to set about reintroducing a new generation to some of what's been lost.

Moving on to a quirk in the wording… why *nine*? Why wasn't it a nice round *ten* stitches saved, for instance? Well, there are two reasons: one logical and one poetic.

Logically, there *is* an implied ten stitches in the proverb as stated. That is, waiting to fix a tear may require ten stitches down the road—thereby "sav[ing] nine," since one is still required even if you act immediately.

But the greater reason is for the sake of making the adage easier to say and remember. You see, "time" and "nine" are what's referred to as *approximate rhyme* (and also *assonance* for you language nerds like me). Interestingly enough, Fuller himself draws attention to this very proverb—as well as another you'll recall from Chapter 5—to illustrate why such a device is so genius:

> *Because verses are easier got by heart,*
> *and stick faster in the memory than prose;*
> *and because the ordinary people use to be*
> *much taken with the clinking of syllables;*
> *many of our proverbs are so form'd, and*

> *very often put into false rhymes; as 'A stitch*
> *in time may save nine' [and] 'Many a little*
> *will make a mickle.' This little artifice, I*
> *imagine, was contriv'd purposely to make*
> *the sense abide the longer in the memory,*
> *by reason of its oddness and archness.*

And as if that weren't enough, the letters of this little gem of a proverb can also be rearranged to form an eerily apropos anagram:

"**T h i s   i s   m e a n t   a s   i n c e n t i v e .**"

(Still) **TRUE**

"A stitch in time saves nine" applies to more than just socks.

Toward making this point palpable, remember that roommate of mine, Seamus, from the opening of the chapter? Allow me to pick up where I left off. There I was, aghast, having just opened a portal to the Amityville Horror. The stacks of defiled plates. The rotting meat. The mother lode of maggots that had burgeoned into a wriggling swarm of black flies. All caught up? Perfect.

Well, no sooner had my brain assimilated the surreal scene for what it was than I slammed the door shut. I stuffed bath towels (and you'd better believe they were *his, not mine*) into every possible escape space. Next, I began tacking a bed sheet (again, *his*) into the ceiling around the entryway until I had effectively cordoned off The Zone. Once the quarantine was complete, I called

Seamus at work, insisting that he make whatever excuse he must to his boss and come home immediately to deal with the crisis. Fortunately for him, he only worked down the street.

About a quarter-hour later, in waltzed Seamus, grinning. I, on the other hand, was not. I ushered him into the antechamber I'd created, dropped the sheet-curtain behind him and simply said, "Please don't come out again until they're gone."

First to emit from the room was a perplexed swearing bout as Seamus took in the scene for the first time. Then I heard one of the windows skittering open. But the screens in the apartment were immovable fixtures, and Seamus apparently realized that this strategy would not work. Moments later, he emerged again. He still wore the same grin, but fear was evident in his widened eyes. "I'm going to go back to work to get some tools," he said, having the gall to add, "I don't know how this happened." Twenty minutes later, he returned with an industrial shop-vac; and for the next hour or so, I was forced to listen to the continued buzzing, the swearing, and the thud of soft bodies bouncing along tubing as they were sucked into oblivion.

Now, I don't know about *you*, but this seems like an awful lot of "stitches" to resolve a problem that could've been avoided with just *one* stitch. After all, it's pretty simple to wash *one* dish and *one* fork and *one* knife after finishing each dinner, rather than leaving them to fester for weeks.

I concede that this story is revolting. And yet before we recoil in horror at Seamus, don't we *all* have a tendency to leave certain parts of our lives ignored or untended until they become their own little horror shows?

I'll tiptoe into this with a lighter topic, so that you can acclimate to the deeper waters ahead. Let's talk about *cleaning*. For some, the thought of cleaning *what currently needs to be cleaned* is enough to give you hives. So you put it off another day. Or until next weekend. Or until the spring. But the funny thing about dirt and clutter is... it just gets dirtier and more cluttered. I'm certain that I've never yet seen a mess clean itself, due to that pesky second law of thermodynamics and all.

I'll be honest with you. I just don't have the time to thoroughly clean my house the way it needs to be cleaned. I don't have housekeeping services, either. Yet my home remains neat as a pin.

Curious as to how I manage it? My strategy is one you now already know: "A stitch in time..."

It's so simple, it's laughable. But whenever I see something that could be cleaner, I just stop in my tracks—and *clean it*. Just that *one* thing, whatever it may be.

Unlike Seamus, when I use a cup or dish or fork, it takes 15 seconds to wash it rather than just drop it in the sink for an indeterminate "later." Using this plan (if you can even call it that), in 25 years of owning dishwashers, I've never needed to use one.

Similarly, if I notice that the top of the toilet (or a bookshelf, or an end table) is a little dusty, I just grab half a paper towel and clean it—right there and then. And so I never have looming, grueling "cleaning days." I just have one-stitch "cleaning *seconds*" accomplished between whatever else I happen to be doing.

All right, I'm about to take the gloves off. I trust you're ready to get real about those "stitches."

So you're sunk in that college course, and your parents are going to lose it if you don't pass. Don't you dare get mad at that "mean and unfair" professor, or leave them a scathing online review when they refuse to give you extra credit at the eleventh hour to make up for the screwing off you did the entire semester up to that point.

"A stitch in time saves nine."

Rosalie Bradford held the world record as the heaviest woman until 2013, weighing in at over 1,200 pounds at one point. She was immobile, able only to lie in the same bed for more than eight years. Depressed. Suicidal. I am haunted by the thought that there is always one day on a calendar when such a person mentally says, "I'm not getting up today. I'm going to soil myself here." You may not be 1,200 pounds. But then, Rosalie wasn't always either.

"A stitch in time saves nine."

Speaking of health, you know that lump—or mole, or cough, or unmentionable yuck—that you've been avoiding seeing the doctor over? A physician's words don't make a thing true; they only add clarity about what is already there. Waiting, on the other hand, *often* makes a thing worse.

"A stitch in time saves nine."

You know those bad behaviors you let your young children get away with, because it's "cute" or too hard to keep up   with? I promise you, as a lifelong mentor of teens, fifteen is coming—and it won't be cute then.

"A stitch in time saves nine."

And that thing that's been bugging you, or that hurt you've been nursing, or that grudge you've been holding against your spouse? No one *plans* for divorce on their wedding day. "Never go to bed angry" is more than just a quaint and cozy platitude from yesteryear.

"A stitch in time saves nine."

The same goes for unspoken "weirdness" with a friend. Or sister, or mother, or neighbor, or boss, or co-worker— or *anyone* for that matter. Take a deep breath. Bring it up. Do it soon. Believe it or not, speaking an awkward thing out loud immediately drains most of the awkwardness out of it. Always remember that every wedge is only a hair wide on the leading end.

"A stitch in time saves nine."

And please don't miss this: as cliché as it may sound, *the other people in your life really aren't mind readers.* It's up to *you* to let them know of your "one-stitch tears" as they happen, not after you've fretted at them a while. It is neither kind, reasonable, nor fair for you to dump a collected mound of shredded rags on someone and expect them to stitch you back together.

Not TRUE

My best friend, Dib, often quotes something her mom, Carlotta, used to say: "Sometimes, if you ignore a problem long enough, it goes away." This may, at first, sound like bad advice—the *opposite*, in fact, of what this whole chapter has been about. But a closer look reveals that there is also truth to it.

One example that comes to mind is gossip. I know all too well from past experience how tempting it can be, when someone's gums are flapping about you, to pull out the needle and thread, and head out on a stitching spree. *Who heard what? Who believes it? Who else might they tell?* But as I detail in *The Best Advice So Far*, "A fire with no fuel quickly goes out." That is, busybodies thrive on *reactions*. Give them none, and they'll be bustling off to more contentious ground before you can say *tittle-tattle*. However, keep in mind that second law of thermodynamics; according to the law of entropy, any situation that rights itself when left alone—was never a *real* problem to begin with.

This seems a good time to add that *worry* most often is also not a call to start stitching. In terms of our proverbial analogy, worry is rather like stitching a sock that you think *might* rip. And that, of course, may actually cause more damage than you'd hoped to prevent. As Cogsworth quips in *Beauty and the Beast*, "If it's not *bar-r-roque... don't fix it.*"

Furthermore, not every tear needs to be stitched by *your hand*. Trust me, my younger self felt compelled—responsible even—to stitch the world back together. For this very reason, I speak and write often about the pitfalls of letting a messiah complex run amok. Here are just a few of the most helpful realizations I've had along the way:

"Lack of planning on your part does not constitute an emergency on my part."

*Just because I **can** solve a problem doesn't mean I **should**. There are billions of people in the world, many of whom I could theoretically help if I knew them; by extension, it's evident that simply knowing a person, or knowing they have a problem, is an illogical reason for me to feel compelled to fix it.*

Someday, I will be gone. And the world will keep turning without me all the same.

*Everything I say **yes** to simultaneously means saying **no** to something else— perhaps something even more important in the grand scheme of things.*

Fixing someone's problem for them may rob them of the most important lesson they'll ever learn.

I'm not saying we shouldn't help others. Far from it. I preach and practice living a life of compassion, and leaving the world and the people in it better for our having been alive. I'm merely advocating for honing our ability to distinguish who's ripped what, and therefore who should be doing the stitching.

Finally, not everything needs to be stitched *at all*. Just because something is uncomfortable for you or not to your liking doesn't mean it needs to be mended.

Trying to stitch up silence in a conversation may well damage more than it repairs. Filling every space with our own words may sew another person's mouth closed.

Learn to be comfortable with strong emotions that others may express. Trade "There, there, don't cry" for a simple "I'm here"—or better yet, simply being willing to sit quietly with someone for as long as it takes.

Likewise, that angry torrent your teen finally shouts at you in exasperation may set your blood to boiling in the moment; but sew it up with punishment or demands for respect, and you'll likely miss one of the biggest gifts they could give you—the gift of *knowing*.

This is all to say that, *sometimes*, even a single stitch is one too many.

Questions & *A Challenge*

1. Had you ever heard "A stitch in time saves nine" before reading this chapter? If so, in what circumstance(s) have you heard it applied before now?

2. The *(Still)* **TRUE** section of this chapter lists several "gloves-off" examples of areas where a stitch in time could save nine (e.g., study habits, weight gain, health issues, etc.). Did any of these particularly resonate with you? Did other areas in your life come to mind, places where perhaps stitching is overdue?

3. Similarly, the <u>**Not**</u> **TRUE** section discusses some areas where we can tend to start stitching when no stitches are necessary (e.g., setting gossip straight, acting purely out of worry, trying to save people from their own consequences, etc.). Which of these did you most relate to? Did other areas come to mind, circumstances where you realize you need to stop trying to stitch things?

CHALLENGE: Stop as soon as you're done reading this challenge and take immediate action on something you know you've left unstitched for too long already. This may be tending to a chore, apologizing to someone, setting up an appointment, or some other such concrete action. Understand that, depending on how long you'velet this area go untended, the process of fully addressing it may require more than one easy stitch. But your action will leave one less of the "nine," and set you on the path of positive change.

8

moss

FROM GALILEO TO GANDHI, great thinkers through the ages have devoted substantial time and effort to working through difficult concepts, or inconsistencies between established dogma and what they themselves observed to be true about the world around them. Even the Grinch had to puzzle until "his puzzler was sore" before he finally figured out why his seemingly foolproof plan had failed.

That said, I'll ask you to get your puzzler dusted off, because we're about to enter the realm of *paradox*.

We say that a statement or proposition is a paradox if it appears, at first, to contradict established "self-evident" facts, or if it seems to prove a point which is not actually true, or if it contradicts itself but is nonetheless true.

My best friend, Dib, would have read that and started to sweat already, suddenly thrust back in time to a desk in some high school math class with a chalkboard that reads, "Train A, traveling 40 mph, leaves Northboro heading toward Southboro, which is 300 miles away..." I say to Dib and others like her, *no need to panic*. It'll all make sense before we're done here.

Still, for those out there who are like me—who think solving paper-and-pencil logic problems or playing Railroad Rush Hour is a fine way to pass leisure time on vacation—I'll drop a quick paradox on you, to whet your appetite.

There's nothing that'll get heads spinning (or geeks arguing) quite like the theoretical "what-ifs" of time travel. It's a perfect playground for paradox. For instance, most people are at least familiar with the 1985 film *Back to the Future*, in which the main character, Marty McFly, rides a tricked-out DeLorean back in time to ensure his parents meet and fall in love. But this presents an unanswerable conundrum, namely that Marty's influence appears to have been crucial to his parents' union and, hence, his own birth; yet in the "original version of the past," then, his parents *did not* marry without his influence... which means he was never born and thus could not have gone back in time.

Professor David Toomey teaches in my neck of the woods, at UMass Dartmouth. In his 2007 book, *The New Time Travelers*, Toomey poses a similar space-time problem. It goes something like this. Suppose a man buys a copy of *Hamlet*, travels back in time and delivers it surreptitiously to William Shakespeare. Shakespeare, quite taken with it, pulls a shady move. He copies the book out word for word in his own handwriting and passes it off as his own work, gaining credit for it throughout the centuries that follow. Eventually, a copy of it winds up in the time traveler's original timeline—the copy he winds up taking back in time to give to Shakespeare. Well, the question then becomes... who actually wrote *Hamlet*?

If all of that is a bit esoteric for your liking, we need not look to time travel to find the wonder of paradox. Nearly all of us have experienced what seem to be opposite emotions at the same time.

We're happy at a wedding... and somehow also strangely sad.

We love someone deeply… and really can't stand them at the moment.

In my own writing and speaking, I've relayed to audiences with the deepest of conviction that honesty is the best policy. At other times, however, I've just as fervently argued that honesty is not *always* the best policy.

In one single chapter of *The Best Advice So Far*, this was the central advice offered:

"You can always do more—and less—than you thought you could do."

So am I advocating for honesty, or for omission? Doing more with your life, or choosing to do less? And the unabashed answer to these questions would be—*yes*. All of these are simultaneously reflective of my beliefs and experience regarding how to live a grounded, fulfilling and happy life.

Often, admittedly, it comes down to how we define terms. What does "honesty" *mean*, both to me and to my audience, or to the society in which we live? Whom am I *currently* addressing: those who've fallen into complacency, or those who have a habit of trying to save the world?

If you've ever been part of a book club—really any open forum centered on a book, movie, poem or work of art—the most thought-provoking, memorable, and even life-changing discussions come about when viewpoints vary the most. You noted a subtle subtext of racism in the book you've all just read, while Leonard across the room felt challenged to be more attentive in his marriage; and

Janelle saw neither of these, but rather felt moved by the carelessness of humans with our planet. Can't *all* of these takeaways be valid?

Often in life (at least if you're doing it right), meaning must be deciphered and applied on an individual basis. And no single interpretation rises above the rest as "the right one."

TRIED

A rolling stone gathers no moss.

While the origins of this adage are not strictly known, we do know that it predates English, turning up in early Germanic and Latin writings. Most people think of Latin as an ancient language (so ancient, in fact, that it's referred to as a "dead language" nowadays). But in case you're thinking Germany hasn't been around all that long, did you know that Julius Caesar had "Germania" on his list of "Places to Conquer Before You Die," back in the first century A.D. when France was still known as Gaul? So, yeah… it's old.

As it so happens, the first version that translates closely to the English was, in fact, in Latin—recorded circa 1500 by Desiderius Erasmus in his collection known as *Adagia* (or, *Adages*):

Saxum volutum non obducitur musco.

Literally, we'd derive from this "A stone revolving will not be covered by moss."

I realize that I may sound like a broken record by now, but I want to pause here to remember that, while this book is about **tried-and-(still)-true** proverbs, each was originally coined and spoken by a *real person*, just like you and me. *Real* people heard them and discovered practical truth in them, pondered them and passed them on to someone else, and so on and so on until it reached us here today. Likewise, if it weren't for the likes of Erasmus, these pieces of wisdom would never have survived into modern times *at all*. I know it's all too easy to hear an unfamiliar name like Desiderius Erasmus and imagine anything but some vague dead guy or perhaps a marble statue. But he *was* a real person all the same—one who had trials and struggles, dreams and aspirations, accomplishments and disappointments. For that reason, I'd like to give Erasmus a bit more time in the spotlight before moving on.

Let's start with that name: Desiderius. To *him* and the people of his day, it wouldn't have sounded strange at all. But to help you relate, think of him for now as *Desi* (pronounced "Dezzy" like Desi Arnaz, who played Ricky Ricardo on the classic television show "I Love Lucy," and whose own full name was quite the tongue-twister: Desiderio Alberto Arnaz y de Acha III).

His name means "desired one." And I'm glad to know that Desi was desired. After all, his older brother and he were bastard sons of a priest and a laywoman—circumstances hardly smiled upon by the High Church of the late fifteenth century. If that weren't enough stacked against him, both his father and his mother died from plague while he was still a child, leaving him and his brother at the will of a stern guardian within that same condemnatory church system. Having no inheritance to speak of, the boys were sent to the only place that would take them—a strict religious school, which for all practical intents was a monastery. Desi would later only remember the place for its harsh discipline intended solely, in his words, "to teach humility by breaking a boy's spirit." Seeking solace, he fell in love with a friend and fellow student—at the all-male school—after which he found himself unceremoniously expelled, disowned and thrown out on his ear again by his "godly" guardian.

Somehow, in spite of it all, he followed through with becoming ordained as a priest. It was no easy choice to stay within the system he hated; but stay he did, with the hopes of initiating internal reforms. What's more, he never lost his love of learning. And so, with seemingly everything against him, he rose from the ashes as it were and became *the* go-to guy where Latin grammar and translation were concerned. He was unrivaled in his knowledge of the original Greek texts of the Bible. And, because of these accomplishments, he began to earn respect and acclaim not only within the Church but in international academia as well. In essence, he was able to say, "I know this stuff *better than you do*, and I'm telling you that you're off base in how you're living and treating people, and in what you're clutching to as important."

Understand that religion was just the way of things for everyone at the time. But remove that particular context, and you have in Desi the equivalent of Oprah Winfrey. Something about his approach instilled a sense of gentle authority and trust. So when he spoke or wrote, people listened. And while they didn't have social media, they publicly "Liked" and "Shared" what he had to say in the manner of the times, spreading his words far and wide.

Now that you know a bit more about the man behind the words, I trust you'll have adequate context to better appreciate his choice to include this chapter's proverb in his writings. Here, I especially relate. You see, I'm also a thinker and a writer. And my own books and talks and facilitation spring from advice I've been collecting for a long while. But I don't just "push what sells." No, I *only* include those pieces of wisdom that I myself have put to the test and found to work consistently, not just in my own life but in the lives of countless others with whom I've shared them. I'm known for my storytelling; but those stories arise from real-life experiences, lessons learned firsthand. And from what I can tell about our friend Desi, he'd been through enough hardship, and thereby developed such a keen sense of what he held to be true about the world, that I can only believe he *also* incorporated in his written work only those sayings which he'd found personally meaningful and trustworthy.

So what *did* Desi and the people of his day take from "A rolling stone gathers no moss"? If you're old enough to have a concept of what *you* think it means, you may be surprised when I tell you that it's likely the *antithesis* of what was originally intended. To wit, early hearers would have understood the *rolling stone* to have negative connotations—a wanderer, a gadabout, a drifter—while *moss* would have been viewed as benefits that naturally come only to those who stick with things, or who are willing to take up permanent residence in one location.

Interpret this through the mind of Desi as he thought,

"This is true. People need to hear this." It should become easier to make sense of why he *stayed* within a religious system he despised, or why he continued with his pursuit of learning despite the many ills he endured within educational institutions. And certainly, in so doing, his tenacity earned him the benefits of knowledge, skill, wisdom and respect that would never have become his had he quit, given in.

Still, for all Desi's tenacity and determination, he was never able to find the "moss" he longed for. Just as moss covers stones and rough terrain, easing tired feet that may travel that way or serving as a plush carpet upon which the weary could rest, putting down roots is the only way a person can experience the joy, comfort and groundedness that accompany deep and lasting relationships. Just as his childhood was marked by sudden and emotional uprooting and love lost, his adult life was likewise one of itinerancy— and all the more as his prominence grew and he was called upon by the rich and powerful for his expertise. Yet despite the accolades, he garnered just as many "haters," as he refused to bend his convictions, influence or voice in pandering to the interests of the elite. And so, it seems, he lived continually surrounded by people, whisked from place to place—and lonely all the same.

I can't help then but to detect a wistful tone as I imagine Desi at a desk somewhere, surrounded by many some-bodies who felt like nobodies, dipping his pen in the inkwell, then pausing to reflect on his life a moment before setting the words to paper in Latin.

Saxum volutum non obducitur musco.

It's interesting to note that the Latin *saxum* could mean many things, "stone" being but one of them. Additionally, the word could mean a cliff, a wall, a slab of marble, a stone edifice, a millstone—even a tombstone. Likewise, "volutum" could mean not only to roll, but to rotate or revolve, to be turned or overturned, or to be enclosed or enveloped.

It was John Heywood (with whom you should now be well familiar) who proffered the English wording we've come to know: "A rolling stone gathers no moss." Yet I can't help but wonder, given all of the various possibilities of meaning represented by those first two important words, if other translations may have been equally valid:

> An eroding cliff grows no moss.
>
> A crumbling wall has no moss.
>
> A grindstone never knows moss.
>
> A stone continually trod upon grows no moss.
>
> An overturned grave loses its moss.

I'm no Latin scholar. Maybe I'm way off from what Desi and those before him heard. But it certainly rouses my curiosity. And I can't help but note, in the context of Desi's life, that *any* of these interpretations could have held equally poignant meaning for him.

The populace of the day would also have taken another significant meaning from the words "gathers no moss." For it was common for the poor to toil in bogs during the heat of summer, dredging up peat moss—perhaps the least known of fossil fuels. This peat moss would then be formed into rough bricks and dried. It was tedious and grueling work. But these early "fire logs" may well be all the warmth a person had to get them through the frigid months ahead. By analogy then, "rolling stones"—those lacking foresight, unwilling to trade carefree summertime fun for the prudence of timely labor—would be left "mossless" and miserable come winter.

Here's where paradox enters the scene.

There is a small number of rather curious English words that hold the class of *auto-antonym*. By this, we mean that multiple definitions of a single word are actually *opposites* of one another. Think of them as one-word paradoxes.

For example, the word "cleave" can mean *both* "to cling" (e.g., "The frightened child cleaved to his mother") *and* "to split apart" (e.g., "He cleaved the log in two with one swift swing of the ax").

Another auto-antonym is "sanction," which can mean either to "approve/allow" (e.g., "The principal sanctioned the use of remaining sports program funds to buy prom decorations") or to "disapprove/prevent/punish" (e.g., "The corrupt company was sanctioned and fined heavily by the SEC after being found guilty of widespread fraud").

Well, "A rolling stone gathers no moss," as it turns out, is *also* a sort of auto-antonym. For during the intervening centuries, both the subject and the predicate of this adage have taken on meanings completely *opposite* from the original. Whether the changes occurred by degrees or in one fell swoop is undocumented. But somehow, emulating the rolling stone became the aspiration, while "gathering moss" became the state one should avoid. That is, the saying became a rally cry to stay in motion, to follow new dreams and take on new challenges, lest you become set in your ways and grow old before your time. And if applied wisely, this more contemporary meaning is just as sound advice as the obverse. Moreover, I'd submit that making a regular habit of *both* applications can and *should* be the goal. We'll unravel that riddle further on; but for now, all I ask is that you continue to keep an open mind.

I'll share one more uncanny tidbit with you for now, something the originator of this chapter's **tried-and-(still)-true** saying couldn't have known and yet which would, in time, support the duality that would befall the proverb. Remember that while Erasmus ("Desi") recorded the words around 1500, the adage itself had been in circulation via word of mouth for more than a thousand years prior. Those ancient people, then, would have called many things *moss* which actually were not, among them—*lichens*. In fact, the distinction between moss and lichens is a relatively modern discovery, having eluded scientists until the late nineteenth century. As such, early hearers of the "rolling stone" proverb would have observed that some kinds of "moss" (i.e., true moss) protected land and prevented erosion, while other types (i.e., lichens) acted like an acid, slowly eating away at solid rock and, eventually, reducing even the grandest castle to rubble. And so, oddly enough, even *they* would have been troubled by the "paradox" of moss as they understood it—how one thing could be, at the same time, both desirable and destructive. Perhaps it was even this conundrum of observation that led to the shift in the meaning of "A rolling stone gathers no moss."

...&...

What do you say we take a break from the heavy thinking for a bit?

If you've ever wondered how The Rolling Stones chose their band name, or how *Rolling Stone* magazine came by the title, you're in luck. Because I'm about to give you the fascinating lowdown. One thing is for sure: they can both ultimately thank Erasmus and John Heywood, because there is a definitive pathway that leads from those distant beginnings to the naming of each of these world-famous contributors to pop culture.

The first issue of *Rolling Stone* magazine was published on November 9, 1967. It had humble beginnings, selling in black-and-white newspaper format for a quarter per issue—nothing like the glossy, jam-packed magazine today's readers have come to know.

Some have supposed, given the timing of that first issue, that *Rolling Stone* took its name from the hit song "Like a Rolling Stone"—the first track from Bob Dylan's 1965 Platinum album, *Highway 61 Revisited*. However, by that time, the band The Rolling Stones had already been on the scene and making waves for several years. So was it this British Invasion powerhouse that sparked the idea for the magazine?

Well, not exactly.

Michael "Mick" Jagger and Keith Richards, the band's founders and staple members, had known one another since attending grade school together. They fell out of touch as each headed a different direction for college (Jagger pursuing economics, of all things, and Richards art); but years later, at a train station in their old hometown, they ran into one another and reconnected when they discovered shared musical interests—in particular, the music of blues great Muddy Waters.

Keith joined Mick's garage band, Little Boy Blue and the Blue Boys, shortly thereafter. It went nowhere. Members came and went. The name changed a few times. One night, after stumbling on the "magic" mix of members and playing a gig at a larger club of note, a member of the press called to get details. The interviewer, of course, asked, "So what do you call yourselves?" Thing was... they hadn't yet picked a name since the last change-up of members. Put on the spot and wanting to sound like they had it more together than "Uh... we don't know yet," Richards fervently began making bug eyes and pointing to an object that happened to be lying on the apartment floor—Muddy Waters' 1950 single, *Rollin' Stone*, which featured the A-side track "Rollin' Stone." And that was all the thought that went into the naming of a band that would go on to become a legend.

This takes us back in time to another "Mick" of sorts, namely McKinley Morganfield, a.k.a Muddy Waters. And his track "Rollin' Stone" makes abundantly clear that *he* took the reference from the proverb.

Verse one has him boasting the benefits of being a "catfish," able to swim the whole ocean of women as he pleases. The second verse gets more personal, offering a glimpse of his philandering with a woman whose husband has just left. But then verse three takes a sudden turn toward the rueful feeling inherent in the early understanding of the proverb; and by verse four, he admits the weariness of the very lifestyle he's touted:

> *"Feel that I could lay down, oh, time ain't long…"*

It's certainly a lot of ground to cover in a three-minute song, particularly for a blues song with oft-repeated lyrics. Yet in the space of those four short verses, Waters' blues style and gritty lyrics serve as the perfect melting pot for blending both the old meaning of the famed proverb and the new.

Whether this weaving of past and present interpretations was Waters' intention or just dumb luck, it's pretty remarkable against the history of the adage.

This all still leaves one of the leading questions from this section unanswered: Whom does *Rolling Stone* magazine credit with the name they chose? And the answer is… *everyone*. From their first issue:

> *Muddy Waters used the name for a song he wrote. The Rolling Stones took their name from Muddy's song. "Like a Rolling Stone" was the title of Bob Dylan's first rock and roll record. We have begun a new publication reflecting what we see are the changes in rock and roll and the changes related to rock and roll.*

And for those in the know (which now includes *you*), they most definitely also acknowledge that the Muddy Waters song and album title hailed from our **tried-and-(still)-true** proverb:

> Rolling Stone *is not just about music, but also about the things and attitudes that the music embraces. We've been working quite hard on it and we hope you can dig it. To describe it any further would be difficult without sounding like bulls**t, and bulls**t is like gathering moss.*

(*Still*) TRUE

Our earlier *coup d'œil* into the life of "Desi" Erasmus certainly speaks volumes regarding the truth of this chapter's proverb: "A rolling stone gathers no moss." Here, I want to expand on those lessons, to acknowledge and further explore the paradox these words hold—the *many truths*, if you will.

Erasmus moved a lot, and much of that not by choice. I can relate. I've lost track of the number of moves my family made when I was young. What I can tell you, however, is that it was enough times to have prompted me to stay in one home for over twenty years as an adult before I could even *think* about packing another box. Having experienced the same kind of whiplash due to the constant uprooting, my mom still has various stuff in boxes from thirty-some-odd years back, for fear that the moment she unpacks them, she'll wind up having to move again.

I realize my family's situation was anomalous. I *can* say that although we changed residences far too often, our "sphere" stayed more or less the same. The "next place" was always located within a 10- or 12-mile radius, one within which nearly all of our extended family also lived. My older brother and I had one change of schools very early on, while my younger sister and brother had none. And because we all went to a small parochial school, that meant we each attended just *one* school until we graduated. So for all the "rolling" we did from house to house, we never really lost our collection of acquired moss as Erasmus did.

Believe me—there were many, many times I wished I *could* have rolled free from some of that gathered moss, much of which was more akin to lichens. I understand all too well that the "ties that bind" can feel an awful lot like a leash. That "sameness" doesn't mean stability. That familiarity really can breed contempt.

So I identify with the wanderlust that seems to burn incessantly within several friends of mine. Every so often, I've even found myself envying them: their ability to drop everything on a dime, pack up their cars and their lives such as they are, and head off to someplace new and exciting every couple of years. Across the country. Around the world.

Yet over the decades, I've also observed certain similarities among those friends who feel that perennial itch to be anywhere but *here*.

It's no coincidence, I think, that the first talk of "maybe moving" almost always comes on the heels of comments about feeling unappreciated at the job. Or during an unresolved conflict with a friend. Or when yet another romance ends abruptly.

In short, that feeling of being *special* as the newest kid on the block wanes. But that's easily remedied. After all, there are many other blocks in the wide world.

Upon arrival at each new place, and perhaps for the first two months, I hear no end of how incredible *this place* is, how open and friendly *these* people are, how much better it is than the last place. Everyone loves them. Conversations are scintillating. The sun is somehow always shining in their photos, and their smile is a mile wide.

By month four, however…

"This place is lame. It's a cesspool. Everyone here is so fake and stuck-up and annoying. And it hasn't stopped raining in three weeks."

And then the ants start invading the pants once again.

I can't help but recall the well-known words: "No matter where you go, there you are." That is to say, if you always seem to be landing smack dab in the middle of the worst of life—the real problem may not lie *out there*.

Building meaningful relationships takes effort, patience, creativity, compromise—things that happen little by little, not all at once. No matter how easy it may appear for someone else to meet new people, strike up conversation, or be the life of the party, forging *real and deep and lasting* relationships just plain takes *time*. And that holds true for *everyone*: introverts, extroverts and everyone in between.

Extend those same principles to the work world.

I mentioned my grandparents in previous chapters. Allow me to tell you a bit more.

My grandfather on my mom's side was the youngest son of a hardworking, no-nonsense immigrant family from

Poland. Born in 1923, he spent the majority of his childhood and adolescence in the thrall of the Great Depression. A decade into the worst economic crisis the U.S. had ever known, and with no relief in sight, the burden became all the heavier when Germany attacked the homeland from which young Alfred's family had come. Over the next two years, the war spread until the United States itself had no choice but to engage. When the draft was enacted, Alfred enlisted in the Navy, which at least afforded him some modicum of choice, since conscripts were automatically assigned to the Army. In a whirlwind before deployment, he married his teen sweetheart, Beatrice. Then, he headed out to sea—and to the unknown.

When the War ended, Al returned to reunite with a bride he hardly knew anymore and to meet his first daughter, Barbara (my mom). And just like that, at barely 21 years of age and still reeling from the atrocities he'd witnessed overseas, he was thrust into the responsibilities of being a family man.

He quickly found himself a job with the Readville Railroad out of Hyde Park, Boston. Hours were long. Hands were calloused. But his dependability, discipline and work ethic soon landed him in a supervisory role. And he'd have stayed with that one company for the long haul had he not broken his back while literally trying to stop a runaway train.

No sooner had he recovered from spinal fusion surgery (and in reality, *before* he had fully recovered, as was his way), he was back out in the workforce. Though he could no longer perform his previous tasks at the railroad, he could *work*. As far as he was concerned, "If you can walk, you can work." Pain be damned. It was with this resolve that he limped his way into the Bird Company, where he served as a foreman for both their machine branch and their roofing branch until he retired.

Two jobs in the course of a lifetime. Three if you count the Navy.

And he only ever moved his family *once* after returning home from war.

You may be thinking that I've paid homage to my Grampa here by way of contrast to those earlier friends who can never seem to stay in one place long; that his constancy is to be admired and emulated, while change is to be eschewed. And you would be exactly…

…*wrong*.

OK, maybe not *exactly* wrong. But not right, either.

Ah, the beauty of paradox.

There is nothing morally better or worse about having had ten jobs in five years, as opposed to hunkering down with one employer for decades. And as I've always maintained, *why* is far more important than *what*. In other words, context is key.

During the Depression, if you were offered a job, you took it. Whether it was at the mills, on the docks or in the mines was irrelevant. There was no consideration as to whether the work was fulfilling, whether you felt you belonged, or whether it was a viable step on the career path you'd always dreamed of. *Working meant eating*. It was as simple as that.

Upon returning from overseas, structure was my grandfather's friend. It had, in a very real sense, saved him during the chaotic nightmare of war. And men, particularly veterans of the day, didn't talk about their feelings. One didn't come home from work and vent. It was "How was your day, Dear?"… "Oh, fine, fine. Yours?" And that was that. For my Grampa, it was usually even less, with an eyebrow raise and wry grunt sufficing. Like a good soldier, you did your job to the best of your ability and without complaint because that was your duty.

Add to that being a father of six, approaching middle age with a broken back. Is it any wonder that his stone never rolled far?

Was his way of doing things worthwhile? For *him*, the answer is a resounding *yes*. Routine served as an anchor for him. Job *security* was just that for him—a safety blanket to a man who'd grown up in unpredictable and tumultuous times. He was well-respected by the crewmen who worked under him. And he earned a respectable wage, enough to provide for the needs of his family.

Yet it's undeniable that *fear* was also an underlying part of the immovability (one might even say rigidity) of the rock that was my grandfather.

Do I *wish* he hadn't known the prejudices that came with being from an immigrant family, with parents who never learned to speak English?

That he'd been able to grow up without the ever-present chokehold of poverty and financial unrest?

That he could have escaped the trauma of war that forever changed his outlook on life and relationships with the people closest to him?

That perhaps he'd lived in a different decade, where a man's emotional well-being wasn't taboo, where he might have received counseling without stigma?

Absolutely.

And might a change in any one of those areas have caused him to make different career decisions, to experience a little more freedom to take risks?

Most likely.

But the fact is that, for all the wishes in the world, he *didn't* live in another era or under different circumstances. His life was *his life*. And his choices were necessarily shaped by *that* reality. And so the moss *he* gathered felt right for *his* stone.

Of course, there are infinite *other realities* that exist between and around those of the perpetual gypsy and the inveterate company man. And each of us is living a unique one.

To illustrate this by highlighting just a couple of factors, the Great Depression is long past. And at the time I'm writing this book, there is no war draft. So the way in which American youth of today approach their futures is a far cry from what it was in my grandfather's day.

It still strikes me as odd that we pressure today's kids to set in stone at 17 or 18 what they want to do with the rest of their lives (and to accept the quarter-million-dollar debt that accompanies that commitment). How could they possibly have gained enough experience or world knowledge yet to even know what the options are? I've been witness to more kids than I can count jumping into pre-med courses just because their father was a doctor. Or gritting their teeth in accounting because "our family have always been accountants." Or muddling through engineering because someone once told them they'd be good at it. Or joining the military because they couldn't think of anything else and "you have to do *something*," rather than because they'd carefully thought it through.

For that matter (and parents, please don't write me mean emails for saying so)... I don't believe college is even the best path for every kid. The important thing is to be a *learner*, not necessarily a *student*. And there are endless ways to learn.

I myself do many things well, skills I've learned by various means along the way: songwriting, composing and singing; computer programming, web design and graphic design; photography; publishing and layout; speaking several languages, and more. I've learned them on my own through reading books, having conversations, following my curiosity, asking lots of questions, observing, availing myself of free online materials and apps. Heck, many things I've mastered through just sheer experimentation. And I'm paid a pretty penny for my collective expertise in many of these areas—none of which were taught as part of my formal education.

Youth is the ideal time to explore. To dabble. To *find out*. Having been a mentor of teens and young adults for three decades now, I actually *encourage* young people to be "rolling stones" for a while—to try as many different things as possible before making any permanent decisions. Date around. Travel if possible. Hold off on declaring that major. What may seem like isolated skills and information can very well combine to form a fulfilling career that had never even been on the radar.

And yet, while I advocate for keeping an open mind and willingness to adapt—an approach to life that in some ways projects, "I still don't know what I want to be when I grow up"—I just as firmly believe in striving for excellence before moving on, in seeing something through even when it gets hard. At some point, if we don't allow our stone to cease its rolling, mere dabbling leaves us, at best, a "jack of all trades, master of none." At worst, which is more often the case, we can actually train ourselves to become chronically *dissatisfied and restless*, always chasing the next temporary high.

Let's take things even further, beyond residence or résumés to *relationships*.

To teens, let me start by saying that, despite what you may feel during your senior year, most friends from high school won't be friends for life. A few may be. But you'll all grow, and that often means growing *apart*. Then, if you do decide to go to college, you'll meet more new people than you can possibly keep up with. Feel free to let your stone roll, and don't carry guilt if you lose some moss along the way. You *will*. And that's OK. It's perfectly normal.

That said, as we get older, if our circles are still constantly changing due to drama in the way of squabbles, unresolved conflicts, shifting allegiances and the like, some self-reflection is probably in order. Yes, there are times in life when the most healthy decision you can make, however difficult it may be, is to let certain people *go*. But if every stone around you is rolling nonstop, it's likely time for you to exit the avalanche, roll on over to some level ground and *settle down*. By that, I don't necessarily mean marriage. I mean choosing quality people to share your life with—people who reflect the values you hold and the kind of life you aspire to live. For me, one of the biggest benefits of getting older has been the ability to devote continually less time and energy to relationships marked by upheaval, and continually more time to a select group of friends who are known for peacefulness, joy, generosity, laughter and love of all things good. People I'd trust with my bank information or my email account passwords, and who would trust me with theirs. That's the kind of moss I'm all too happy to be gathering.

Not **TRUE**

Settling down doesn't have to mean stagnation. Thanks to the mystical power of paradox, much as a tree can continue to spread its branches without pulling up roots, we can choose to stay even as we continue rolling. We can enjoy travel without moving. We can explore without ever leaving the neighborhood. We can follow our curiosity without needing to go anywhere at all.

Mind you, staying put doesn't guarantee that you *will* have strong relationships. Sadly, there's a whole phenomenon I call the "lonely internet culture" that makes this point abundantly clear: people with fingertips on autopilot, scrolling through their social media accounts, posting perfect pics and quips—all from the same bed or couch they were curled up on the night before and the one before that, mere voyeurs to the real world going on right outside their door.

By the same measure, the careful wanderer may very well collect his own moss by way of language immersion, broadened scope of experience, a firmer grasp of national and world history, or a deepened sensitivity to and appreciation for diverse cultures and peoples. In fact, regarding the more common contemporary interpretation of a "rolling stone," a conscientious person may roam *and yet* remain grounded at the same time. If we remain self-aware, we can make new friends in new places, without abandoning old ones. We can travel often, and still have a place we call *home,* to which we return.

How much *your* stone should roll, and which moss you should gather or shake loose, will always come back to an honest look at yourself, your motives and intentions, building on the foundation laid in Chapter 1: "Know thyself."

Do you stay in your hometown, determined to find the undiscovered beauty already around you? Or would a fresh start and clean slate best help you at this stage of your life?

Can you give that job another year or so, on the lookout for what else you might yet be able to learn there? Or have you gleaned from it all you can at this point, as it fits within your big-picture plan?

Should you work through the current issues with that friend? Or have you thought long and hard about the relationship and realized it's no more than a drain that's sapping your happiness?

Is the choice to move an indication of running *to* something... or merely running *away from* something?

Or is your choice to stay based on true contentment... or complacency?

In the end, the right answer will come down to your adeptness at distinguishing the moss from the lichens.

Questions & A Challenge

1. How did you do with reaching back through five centuries and empathizing with "Desi" Erasmus? Were you able to see him as a real person? Whether you said yes or no, how might you benefit from an increased ability to empathize with people you don't know and whom you'll likely never meet? Are there any recent circumstances when you've been able to do this?

2. Do you easily identify with either interpretation of "A rolling stone gathers no moss": the caution to settle down a bit in order to gain skills, knowledge or deeper relationships; or the caution to keep living, growing, trying new things so that you don't grow old before your time? If not, in the vein of the Muddy Waters song lyrics, do you find yourself somewhere between these two extremes? Or do you feel the current state of your "stone and moss" is just where it should be? And if the latter, has this always been true about you?

3. Are there any specific choices you are currently facing where you're having trouble "distinguishing the moss from the lichens"? What could you do that might bring some added clarity to that decision?

CHALLENGE: This chapter offers you another choose-your-own-adventure challenge! Pick one.

A. If you most identify as someone whose stone has been rolling too much lately, this challenge is for you. Other than necessary activities like school, work or the like, don't go out this week. But don't just scroll through social media or watch television by yourself. "Gather some moss" by inviting friends over for dinner, conversation or games; call and catch up with family members; do a jigsaw puzzle with the family. Choose something that adds real value to your down time.

B. If you most identify as someone whose stone needs to roll more, this is your challenge. In the next week, choose three activities that you don't normally do—and do them. Have dinner out or go bowling with a friend; take a weekend trip; spend some time walking in nature. Choose something that shakes loose the feeling of "the rut."

C. If you're not sure where you fit with "A rolling stone gathers no moss," or if you feel you're at a good place with the amount your stone is currently rolling and the moss you've been gathering, this challenge is for you. We can all benefit from following our curiosity or trying something new, whether we stay home or go out into the world. In the next week, collect as many new experiences as you can: try some new foods or make a new recipe; learn a quick new skill; visit a store in town that you've never been to (even if you don't need their wares or services); take a new route to work or home again. Simple or complex doesn't matter; new is the key. When the week is up, reflect on how it felt to explore these new things.

9

gone

"GONE BUT NOT FORGOTTEN."

Of itself, it's a charming sentiment, if a bit quaint and overused. In fact, it's so common that it's even got its own shorthand in texts and social media: **GBNF**. Yet even in its starkness, it fails to capture the gritty reality of loss and remembrance.

My Grampa passed away in 2010 at the age of 86, after a four-year battle with Alzheimer's.

I remember the last family reunion we had before things went sideways. It was summer, as always, and Grampa seemed his usual self. Walking with the lopsided gait he'd had since before I was born, which was not unlike—and I mean this fondly—that of an orangutan. Speaking little, just enough to make sure everyone had enough root beer or that the potato salad ("ba-day-da salad" as he said it) stayed covered in the sun, or to tell the younger grandkids to stop being so rough with the garden gnomes.

It seems like the next day, I'd heard that he was calling some of my cousins by the wrong name. Within hardly more than a week, he was wandering out in his underwear, thinking he needed to drive somewhere. Then he became belligerent and violent, and hard decisions had to be made.

Just like that, we'd lost the man we'd always known. There truly was no time for goodbyes.

Four years is a long time to watch the replica of someone you love still breathing, but looking out of eyes you no longer recognize. Eyes that no longer recognize you.

Nana had the hardest time accepting that the man she married wasn't the one shouting at her, saying things his healthy self would never have said or even thought. Telling her he hated her. Still, she went and sat with him in the nursing home every day, speaking to him as if everything were right as rain. Talking about household chores and who was keeping up with them "until he came home."

Over the course of those four years, there were many days they weren't sure he was going to make it through the night. He'd stop eating. Stop drinking. Stop responding. Each time, my mother would call and let us know that "this could be it." And we'd go to the nursing home. Then, when all hope was lost and we were holding our collective breath, his eyes would fly open and he'd say he wanted a hot dog.

I remember my mother's call on the day he died. There was something in her voice, despite all the times before, that made my stomach feel as if it were icing over. Somehow, I knew.

I remember every detail of the day Grampa died. Twenty or so of our family were gathered around his bedside in the hospital room. I was surprised how thin he'd become so quickly. He was not conscious. Yet throughout the long hours, Nana sat by his side, holding his hand, sometimes quiet and sometimes talking to him as if he were wide awake and they were on a picnic. She never left to take a break. To eat. Not even to use the restroom. She stayed.

My uncle lived out of state. Another of my aunts had been putting off a visit to Michigan for years, fearing she'd somehow wind up away when the time finally came.

Ironically, she'd decided a few days earlier to make that trip. "We're trying to reach them, Dad. Hang on, don't go. They'll call back," another aunt repeated, her face pale and waxy from the tears. A phone was held up to Grampa's ear as his distant son and daughter tried to find the words to say goodbye to a father they weren't even sure could hear them.

Shortly after those calls ended, Grampa's vital signs shifted drastically. He began simply fading away. His breathing and pulse finally became so faint that a nurse with a stethoscope was required, in order to know whether he was breathing at all. Around his bedside, each of us placed a hand on him, or on my grandmother or on someone nearby. His sheet-draped leg was cold beneath my fingers.

Nana had been a rock, unwavering, strong for him. But in the silence surrounding those last moments, she cracked. I'd never seen anyone cry the way she did. Calling out loudly for him by name: "No, Al! No! It's supposed to be me and you. It's always been me and you, for my whole life. I was 17. Seventy years now. I can't do this without you. I don't know how. Take me with you, I don't want to stay here without you…"

The attending nurse did not interrupt to announce time of death. She simply caught my mother's eye, shook her head almost imperceptibly—then silently left us to grieve.

Nearly a year passed before Nana began to laugh again. I remember because it was Memorial Day. I'd almost forgotten what her laughter sounded like.

In the years since then, healing happened. Memories of Grampa began to bring smiles more often than the sting of tears. We could joke about his walk or his ways without feeling disrespectful, much as we did when he was alive. We could quote his quotables and feel his presence in them again.

We lost Nana in the late winter of 2019, at the age of 94. And so we once again began the gradual process of letting go even while holding onto all she meant—all she still means— to us.

Nana and Grampa are *gone but not forgotten*.

I tell you these intimate details of my grandparents' passing in hopes of bringing some meaning back to the words. Yet that's not the end goal. In fact, "gone but not forgotten" isn't even the central saying for this chapter. It's only a lead-in to the *real* topic at hand: clarity through contrast, if you will. You see, remembering a loved one who's passed can be healthy. Healing. It can instill a sense of groundedness, help us make peace with the past even as we move forward.

But there are other imposters of "gone but not forgotten" that are not so noble and hardly healthy. They're insidious soul drains, slowly replacing lifeblood with embalming fluid. They'll leave a doppelgänger where you once stood, and you'll never even know you've been replaced.

TRIED

Let bygones be bygones.

"Gone but not forgotten" reminds us to hold on.

"Let bygones be bygones," on the other hand, exhorts us to *let go*.

The first approximation of these words appeared in 1562, within the pages of *Proverbs and Epigrams*, by John Heywood (who also brought us "Haste makes waste" from Chapter 6). Here, we are dropped into a dialogue between a husband and his wife whom he has clearly wronged:

> Well, well! (quoth she), whatever ye now say,
> It is too late to call again yesterday.
> Wife! (quoth he), such may my diligence seem
> That th 'offence of yesterday I may redeem;
> God taketh me as I am, and not as I was—
> Take you me so too, and **let all things past
> Pass...**

I'll admit, my first response to this man is not favorable. Is he merely using religious guilt to worm his way back into good graces after an affair (or several)? And even if he *were* truly remorseful, is his wife then beholden to act as if it had never happened—to "forgive and forget" as it were (lines Heywood proffers just a few lines earlier in the same book, spoken by the same husband, by the way)?

While I can attest to the personal freedom that comes with forgiveness (and will do so later in this chapter), and while I don't believe that letting something go always means letting someone *back in* (also ahead), if this one passage were all we had by way of history on this **tried-and-(still)-true** saying, I'd probably have left it out altogether. Too complicated. And it's not really at the heart of what the saying has come to mean.

It wasn't until a Scottish preacher by the name of Samuel Rutherford took to pen nearly 75 years later that the more familiar form emerged:

> **"Pray that byegones betwixt me and my Lord may be byegones."**

However you feel about religion, I believe the more you discover about the man who wrote this, the less inclined you'll be to bristle at his words.

First, I think we somehow get this idea that "old words" must all have come from "old people." And yet this book, and this year's graduation speeches, and birthday cards, and the emails and texts that we're continually sending *right now* will also, someday, be "old." But that doesn't mean *we* were when we wrote them.

No, the Samuel who wrote those words was just a young man with a head full of dreams, setting out to make a difference in the world the best way he knew how. One elderly man from his town said of Sam, "…he seemed to be altogether taken up with everything good, and excellent, and useful…" And it seems this is how he was known by many in his day: diligent, caring, humble.

That is until he began somewhere along the way, in the earnestness of his youth, to dare say aloud, "Hey, I think some of the established ideas we've been holding to might not be quite right." Then all bets were off.

And his thinking wasn't some pie-in-the-sky theology, either. This was a young man who'd known grief, deeply and often. All but one of his children died young. The love of his life also died by the time he was 30. And soon after his mother moved in to comfort him, she also passed away. It's no wonder then that, for all the good he sought to do for others, he himself struggled with depression.

And what was the response of the powers that be (or that *were*)? Compassion? Understanding? Taking him under wing?

No. It was essentially "Shut up or get out." And when Samuel *didn't* shut up, they got him out. Straight-up exiled him.

So here's a guy who undoubtedly has been horribly *wronged*. Wronged by the people he looked up to and trusted. Wronged by life. Wronged by *God*, if you want to go there. And yet it is *this* man who brings into being such words:

"Pray that byegones betwixt me and my Lord may be byegones."

Takes on new meaning, doesn't it? Is this a plea for forgiveness, perhaps for understandable spells of bitterness and doubt… or was it an *offering* of forgiveness, by a man who knew somehow, despite everything, that he would be in an even more pitiful state if he allowed the past to eat away at his continual present?

...&...

At face value, letting bygones be bygones may seem at odds with the sentiment behind "gone but not forgotten." Rutherford's context, however, makes it clear that "bygones" aren't just *any* people or circumstances from the past.

Bygones involve *negative* experiences.

In addition, the opening word—*let*—indicates an admonish-ment. Today, we might simply say, "Let it go." When someone speaks these words to us, we know exactly what the "it" is based on context. Furthermore, such a reminder would be wholly unnecessary if it were reflective of most people's first thought or inclination. For instance, we wouldn't need to say "*Let* your brother play the video game for a while" to someone who was already sharing. Similarly, we wouldn't say "*Let* love in" to someone who was demonstrating an openness to love in the first place.

All this is to say that, for most of us, following this bit of advice will be *hard work* that may require breaking life-long thought patterns.

(Still) TRUE

Growing up, I went to a highly dysfunctional parochial school.

The school was characterized by excessive, unfounded and often absurd rules—all alleging to have been "the will of God."

No dancing. Dancing of any kind at any time and for any reason—even at a wedding—was grounds for punish-ment or expulsion.

Girls could not wear pants or shorts *anywhere*, including at home. Even while playing sports, they were required to wear shin-length polyester culottes with tube socks pulled up underneath so that no skin was showing. And even that was considered a "liberal" concession.

Denim was decried as "the devil's material" and forbidden to be worn at any time, in or out of school. If someone reported that they'd seen you wearing jeans on a Saturday, you'd be hauled into the principal's office come Monday morning.

Hair must not be colored, styled or cut in accordance with modern fashions. And boys' hair was required to be what we called "white-walled": a half-inch minimum off the ear, shirt collar and eyebrows. In eighth grade, I entered a music competition between like-minded parochial schools. After months of arduous practice, I took the stage and played Rachmaninoff's *Prelude Op. 3 No. 2 in C♯ Minor* nearly flawlessly (the same piece I mentioned in chapter 6). The judges awarded me an overall score of zero and disqualified me, scrawling "hair touching eyebrow" as the only note on my judging form.

What's more, parents were required to sign over unrestricted rights of corporal punishment, which meant that teachers had free reign to physically strike students whenever and however they wanted with no recourse... a situation of which many took full advantage.

The general rule of corporal punishment (when teachers bothered with a "rule" at all) was that the offending party would be brought to the principal's office to be "paddled." The paddle was a square wooden board with a handle, much like a bread board. It hung on a hook by the glass-topped desk when not in use—a reminder to all that it could just as easily be taken down at any time. The student was required to assume "the position": toes and heels together, bent over with hands braced on knees. The adult would then administer 10 strikes with the paddle—*hard*. If the student at any time broke "the position" by taking a hand off a knee or stepping forward the slightest bit to maintain balance, the ritual would begin again with the count reset to one. Since it was a K-12 school and paddling applied to all, most students—particularly those in kindergarten and elementary school—didn't escape with the minimum 10.

I'm only able to give you a glimpse here. The full reality was more horrifying than I'm able to capture in short order. Yet this warped and sadistic environment was the norm for us.

And within this system, I remained a model student.

I was a perfectionist. So getting the highest marks, and remembering and keeping all rules, were no great challenge.

In sixth grade, I received my first and only paddling. The reason was that I had forgotten my lunch at home, and, therefore, was allegedly trying to draw attention to myself, which was prideful (I kid you not).

I did not flinch.

I did not stumble.

I did not cry.

That teacher could beat me, but she was not going to break me. I was not giving her the satisfaction.

Twenty-some-odd years later, I ran into that teacher in a grocery store aisle. I had not seen her in the interim. Even more than two decades later, she sneered at me with derision and said, "Well, well, well… it looks like at least *one* of the Tyler kids managed to make it to adulthood."

I stopped and drew in a slow breath. I smiled a tight, thin line of a smile that held no mirth. I looked her square in the eye and replied, calling her by her first name (changed here): "Winifred, do you know what I remember about having you as a teacher? I don't remember a single lesson or fact you taught. I don't remember a word of encouragement or praise. I don't remember any joy of learning. I only remember that you paddled me when I was 11... for forgetting my lunch."

She was unmoved. She arched an eyebrow, lowered her lids and pursed her lips, replying matter-of-factly, "I didn't paddle you for forgetting your lunch."

I stood my ground, calmly. "Yes... you did," I countered. "It was the only time I was ever paddled in that place. I remember it well."

"Oh, *I paddled you*," she retorted smugly. "I remember it just as well. But it wasn't for forgetting your lunch. That's just what I *told* you it was for. I really paddled you because I didn't like you going around thinking you were so perfect."

Those of you with any empathy intact may be experiencing something akin to anger while reading all of this. And that's merely your *vicarious* response. Imagine actually having been me and the other students who attended that school at the time (keeping in mind that I fared much better than most).

Sadly, many of those who attended the school during that time—all of whom are now well into middle age— are *still* angry. For many, their entire lives since then have been tethered to the bitterness and anger that accumulated during those years, so many decades ago. On the rare occasion that we might see one another anymore in life, caustic rehashing and sneering recollections of "those days" are the only topic of conversation. It's a perpetually damaging misapplication of "Gone but not forgotten."

If I'm being honest, that was me until sometime in my early twenties. I was angry. All the time. It wasn't the kind of anger that flares up when someone cuts you off in traffic. It was a deep anger that crept like briars through my stomach. I often missed consecutive meals without realizing it (once for about 10 days in college, landing me in the hospital in serious condition), because the gnawing pangs of perpetual bitterness overshadowed even the natural feeling of hunger.

I was on the phone one afternoon with my best friend, Dib, and she said something that I knew would wind up in my writing as soon as it left her lips:

"Anger is nothing but a big, fat drain."

She continued, "I could easily allow myself to get wrapped up and angry. But why? It's like that person already caused an upset and... what?... now I'm going to *give* them my peace and happiness, too? No way."

Wise words. And in some respects, very simple ones. Moreover, they're a shining example of the truth that "You *always* have a choice."

I remember when that idea—that, in every circumstance, I had a choice—first became real to me. I was 21. It was the middle of the night. I couldn't sleep. The hooks of anger were pulling taut inside. My mind was doing what it had done so many times before: replaying on loop the ever-lengthening movie of a lifetime of offenses and hurts.

But somewhere in my dark reverie, another "voice" cut in. It almost seemed to be coming from outside of myself, being in such contrast to the seething rancor that held me like a straitjacket:

> "Your anger isn't changing anything. It's not making anyone pay. It's not making anyone sorry. They're sound asleep right now while you lie awake, a wreck. Yes, those people took years of your childhood. That was not your choice. But those years are over. Now, you're *choosing* to give them more hours, more nights, more months, more years— beyond the ones they stole. Those people are no longer able to take your peace and happiness. You're *choosing* to give it away now."

And that voice only further fueled my anger. Or was it panic? Hopelessness?

If I *didn't* remain angry, it felt like I was giving up the fight against people who were 100% in the wrong, like moving on and choosing to be happy… was letting bad people *win*.

But somewhere during those next few hours of inner turmoil, reason won out. I saw it clearly for the first time. My freedom and happiness had been *taken* from me in the past. But now, in the present, I was choosing to continually *give* it away. Day after day… after day.

"Anger is nothing but a big, fat drain."

It doesn't matter what you're angry about. From a horrible boss to a childhood sexual abuser to a presidency, you *always* have a choice. Other people make their choices. And you have the power to make *yours*. Knowing where their choices end and where yours begin is the foundation of peace, of happiness.

The truth I realized was that the past and the hurtful people in it held no actual power over me. Other than some microscopic neurons in your cerebral cortex and eyes, you quite *literally* aren't the same person you were two decades ago, even at a cellular level. So the only power a person from your past has over you is the power you continue to give them *in your mind*.

Of course, the things that eventually become the by-gones that can drive us to bitterness are at some point *current*, even unavoidable in many cases. I'll give one additional example from my own life.

The phone rang at 9:52. Unknown number. I didn't pick up.

At 9:53, a voice message appeared. I listened.

It was "Fabiola from the District Court victim advocacy office," informing me that the case against the woman who had stolen my wallet and fraudulently used my debit card the previous summer was finally being heard that day. It was a short message, which ended by asking me to return the call if there was anything I wanted to add to the case before it went before the judge.

At 9:55—three minutes after the phone had rung—I called back. No answer. I left a message explaining that the local police detective in charge of the case had assured me I'd receive an invitation to appear in court when the woman was tried, but that I'd received no such letter or call. I requested that the case be postponed until such an invitation could be issued allowing me to be present, and I asked that Fabiola call me back.

I continued to call back every 5 or 10 minutes. Answering machine. Answering machine. I left a couple of other messages with details pertinent to the case:

I'd learned that this woman had 19 prior counts of theft and fraud before mine, and yet had never received jail time.

I'd lost not only days of my life trying to rectify the stolen funds with my bank and piece back together the contents of the stolen wallet, but actual money by way of lost work hours and having to order a replacement license. And there were personal items in the wallet—old photos and notes—that could never be replaced.

The woman had committed these thefts with a child of under four years of age in tow, using the boy as part of the con. Involving the child in the crimes, I explained, was modeling to this child that theft was an acceptable way of life.

Do you think me heartless? Did you imagine that I'd have more compassion given my lifelong role as a mentor to youth, many of whom have made poor choices along the way?

Please know that my first response *was* compassion.

Had I learned that the woman had used my bank card to buy baby formula, diapers or food staples, I would have shown up to court and advocated for leniency, even offering her my own help where possible.

But it quickly became clear the day of the incident the previous summer, as I checked my live bank statement, that she was not stealing out of indigence or need. No, she was rushing down my own street (a mark of a seasoned criminal, knowing that purchases near the residence of the victim are less likely to be flagged immediately as fraud), buying cartons of cigarettes here, magazines there, donut gift cards at the next place.

At close to 11:00, Fabiola called back. The case had gone to trial at 10:00, she told me. She was upstairs at the hearing when I'd called back.

I could feel my blood pressure rising.

"Fabiola," I said, "so what you're telling me is that you called me eight minutes before the hearing and immediately hung up the phone and went upstairs—which means you had absolutely no intention of hearing my feedback before the case was tried."

Awkward silence on the phone.

Then the excuses began.

"Well, we sent a letter to you in February."

"I didn't receive any letter. What address do you have?"

"8 Meadow Lane…"

"No, I haven't lived there in over six years. And it's not the address I listed on the police report."

"Oh, well, I'm sorry you didn't receive the letter, but we did send it."

"Yes, you sent it to the wrong address instead of the

one I provided on my victim statement. Are you telling me that the police didn't give you my victim statement? It's not in your case file? Because if that's what you're telling me, I need to hang up with you and go right down to the police department to file a complaint against the detective in charge. Gee, and he seemed so competent…"

"Well," Fabiola hemmed and hawed, "I didn't say we didn't get the report. I just know that we sent a letter to 8 Meadow Lane and didn't hear from you."

"And that is because, as I've said, I don't live there and haven't in a very long time. Are you telling me you didn't receive it back from the post office then? Because after I get done at the police station, it sounds like you're telling me that I need to stop in at the post office and ask why they also screwed up. But what I'm sure of is that you had my phone number, because you called me this morning—eight minutes before the trial."

More awkward silence.

"I was only just able to find your phone number this morning, sir. But good news. The defendant pleaded guilty and received probation."

I took a long, slow breath and let it out.

After 19 priors and involving a young child in her con, the woman had received… ***probation***?

This went round and round for another several minutes with Fabiola refusing to accept any responsibility and telling me there was nothing I could do about it at this point.

I was over it. As politely as I could muster, despite hearing my own heartbeat in my ears, I ended the call with Fabiola.

In my book *The Best Advice So Far*, I present many gems of wisdom that I myself turn to again and again:

> *Misery is a choice.*

> *Worry serves no purpose but to ruin the present.*

> *The sooner you accept that life is not fair, the happier you will be.*

In addition, I write and speak quite a bit about topics like how to navigate regret, banish worry, and let go of anger before it turns into bitterness. But there's some related ground that doesn't get much air time.

I call it *dwelling*.

Dwelling is a bit different from regret, worry or anger. And yet it can involve elements of all of these. It's a sort of nebulous in-betweener. It's good at hiding in the gray area—which is why it tends to go unnoticed for so long.

When dwelling sets in, we tend to find ourselves saying things like:

"I can't focus. I'm distracted."

"I just feel exhausted all the time."

"I feel depressed, but I don't know why."

But these personal expressions speak only about *effects*, not the underlying cause—the roots that lie hidden below the surface, leeching the vitality from the soil of the soul.

I had a conversation recently with a friend I'll call "Ray" here. Ray and I were talking on the phone, and he expressed that he'd been feeling tired and empty for a while. "But," he added, "there's really no reason for it that I can see. Work is fine. The family's good. It just doesn't make sense."

For the next few minutes, we brainstormed together, considering everything from certain vitamin deficiencies to seasonal affect disorder. But I've seen the strangle hold of this peculiar variety of bygone enough times by now to at least pose the question: "Ray, is there any one thought you find your mind returning to frequently—one that makes you feel upset, but that you keep pushing away or minimizing because you don't know what to do with it?"

No sooner had I asked than Ray offered, "Well, yeah… sort of." He told me exactly what it was.

And sure enough… it was a case of dwelling.

Like regret, my friend wondered whether things might have turned out differently in that hurtful situation if he'd somehow known or said or done something he hadn't at the time.

Like worry, he went round in circles about whether he might have some sort of responsibility remaining, to do something that might prevent a similar situation from happening to others in the future.

Like anger, he felt his life had been made more difficult by others' incompetence and mistreatment. But those others were not people he knew personally, and they were only small cogs in the machinery of a much larger broken system.

And so he tucked the situation away until a perennial "later," when maybe it would play out differently somehow, or he'd see whatever he'd been missing that would vindicate himself while finally making sure the wrong-doers got their comeuppance.

Only thing is, for all the mental expenditure, not a thing

had changed in the year between.

I realize I've explained a bit about what dwelling isn't, or what it's like, or what it does to us; but I haven't quite spelled out *what it is*.

As best I can describe it, dwelling is replaying the details of a "bygone"—often one we identify as "unfair"—with the intention of somehow *making* it fair eventually (even if we don't immediately recognize that's what we're doing).

We have "that conversation" again and again, wishing we'd said something smarter.

Or that someone in authority had stood up for us.

Or that we hadn't felt so helpless.

Somewhere in the back of our consciousness, we imagine that our feelings of being wronged will matter "this time" when we rerun the scene, or even that revisiting it again and again will have some kind of cumulative effect.

Or maybe by overexposure, we'll become numb to it and it won't hurt so much.

Dwelling often has a generic, distanced or vague object:

the situation

the system

the government

people / the world

life

...which is why it tends to slip under the radar for so long. Because anger feels like it should have a clear object for us to get mad at. In fact, we may have thought we worked through anger toward a specific person, while continuing to dwell on the situation (e.g., the time we lost, why we didn't see it sooner, how this could have happened to me, or why do things like this *always happen to me*, etc.).

At other times, dwelling centers on an encounter where a stranger or person we'll never see again mistreated us.

And so we don't know what to do with it. No matter how many times we rewrite the script—to rework the characters, plot or lines—it always returns to the same program that aired the first time around.

The good news is that the solution for moving on from dwelling is fairly simple, at least as I've come to practice it. And that solution is the same one I use for just about any of the look-alikes such as regret, worry or anger. Here's my personal prescription for letting bygones be bygones:

I ask myself, "Is there anything I can do about this right now?"

If there is, I do it right away, however small a thing it may be. Yet what I've realized with dwelling—something which distinguishes it from the similar emotions of regret, worry and anger—is that often, all you can do is identify and accept that you are dwelling, and that it isn't getting you anywhere.

If I determine that there is nothing I can do about the issue right now, beyond that acceptance that I've been dwelling,   I ask myself, "Is there anything I can do about this at a later time?"

Often, this turns up a different result from asking whether there is anything I can do immediately. One of the most common times dwelling rears up is in the middle of the night.

So let's say I find myself dwelling again on the court thing at 3:00 in the morning. And I decide that, while I could get out of bed and write a letter, it's probably not wise, seeing that I've got to get up in a few hours. If I find there is something such as this that I can do at a later time, I write down what I can do and when.

You may think this seems like a silly step. But I've found that physically writing down that next step does something in the way of symbolically taking the situation out of my head and making it external. To have the thing I've been dwelling on—and its next possible action point—written safely down and folded up on the bedside table, or added to my phone schedule, assures my subconscious mind that I won't forget.

And so if that dwelling tries to persist, I just focus my thoughts: "It's OK. I wrote it down. I will do something about it at that time." Strangely enough, this allows me to sleep in those wee-hours dwell-spells (or to keep from being distracted during *any* interim, such as work, where I can't address an action point immediately).

If, however, I've answered that there is nothing I can do at the moment and nothing I can do at any time in the future about what I've been dwelling on—and this is the most important step—I make a deliberate and active choice to *let it go*. To let that bygone *be bygone*.

I reiterate to myself that I have done all I can do, and that continuing to give this thing any more brain space and energy is only wrecking perfectly good moments in the present. If I find the scene trying to play itself out again in my head down the road, I shut the thoughts down immediately, reminding myself that I've already put the issue to the test and determined that it is 100% out of my control.

So I don't try to control it.

Not TRUE

Letting bygones be bygones *doesn't* mean that we forget. We may feel absolutely certain that we've sailed past certain hurts into calm waters, only to later find ourselves dashed up against the jagged rocks of emotion by waves that seem to come out of nowhere. Be patient with yourself. Healing is a process, as is forgiveness.

Forgiveness is also not the same thing as *trust*. Nor is letting bygones be bygones somehow proven by being "besties" with those who hurt us. Sometimes, relationships can be restored. Sometimes, they can't—nor *should* they be if we are going to move forward in health.

Sometimes, in fact, the *best* choice for letting bygones be bygones is to remove yourself from the influence of a person or situation altogether. It might be hard. *Really* hard. But often, it's a choice within our power all the same.

Find a different job.

Break up.

Move out.

Get a new roommate.

Turn off the TV.

In addition, keep in mind that "bygones" cover a lot of ground. Bygones may be something that happened two minutes or two *decades* ago. And so, for instance, dwelling can happen throughout the course of a day. Or it can last for weeks, months—even years. The sooner we can identify it for what it is and start shutting it down, the better. Without taking measures to lift the needle from the record, it will play indefinitely, scratching away at our happiness.

In the case of the woman who'd stolen my wallet, and the subsequent failures of the court system, I found myself feeling the weight of the unfairness. I replayed the details as I drove. I felt the tightness in my jaw as I worked with clients, distracting me from giving them my full attention.

A few hours in, I realized I was at the beginning stages of dwelling. And as soon as I recognized it, I put it to my three-step test:

Could I do anything to change the situation right now?
I decided I could not.

Could I do anything about it later?
I considered that I could write a letter to the judge in the case, explaining my experience and the shortcomings of the victim advocacy office. But I decided this would not really change the system or the outcome of the case. And while I could contact the probation officer and follow up each and every month, waiting for the wallet thief to miss a check-in so that I could drag her back into court, I finally determined that this would also not change the woman or the broken system. All it would do is allow the woman's actions to continue to take up more of my peace, happiness and time with negativity.

Having decided that there was nothing I could do now, and nothing of value I could do later—*I just didn't give it any more airplay.*

And every time vapors of it tried to coalesce in the hours and days that followed—to gain momentum through words, images or emotions—I scattered them decisively, stating matter-of-factly, "No, I've already put this one into the 'cannot-control' chute. Done."

I'm here to tell you that being consistent and disciplined with this strategy really works.

That said, I need to mention that there are certain scenarios where you may not want to go it alone in getting past your own bygones:

> You realize that you've been dwelling on the same thing for years—even a lifetime.

> You honestly aren't sure whether you can do anything about the situations now or later.

> There are many different circumstances that come back to haunt you, rather than one or two.

> You suspect that incidents from your past have contributed to persistent and detrimental mindsets or patterns of behavior in the present: bitterness, shame, fear, trust issues.

If any of these special cases sounds like you, the process I've suggested in this chapter still applies. However, you may want to invite help from a counselor in working through the steps and getting to a place where lingering hurt no longer has a hold on you.

Remember, dwelling on bygones (i.e., replaying situations over and over without any change) is 100% wasted energy. It does not tip the cosmic scales in our favor. And not only is it wasted time and energy, it steals from our *one source* of time and energy, leaving us depleted in other areas that *do* matter and that we *could* do something about.

Perhaps worst of all, hanging onto our bygones gives negative experiences a prolonged lifespan, well after the events themselves are over and done with.

The wonderful reality is that the past has no more power over us than what we choose to give it.

Questions & A Challenge

1. Did any specific circumstances, past or present, come to mind that you can now identify clearly as "dwelling"?

2. How easy is it for you to truly let bygones be bygones, such that they no longer control present moments or your state of mind?

3. I outlined my three-step process for letting bygones be bygones (as well as for dealing with regret and worry). What are your own go-to strategies for handling regret, worry or "dwelling"? Have you thought any new thoughts with regard to these things after having read this chapter? (If so, jot them down somewhere you can read them again in the future as needed.)

CHALLENGE: When you become aware that you are dwelling on something this week, make a concerted effort to try the three-step approach from this chapter:

• Can I do anything about it right now? (If so, do it right now.)

• Can I do anything about it later? (If so, write it down with a reminder, and do it at the next available opportunity.)

• If you determine that you can do nothing constructive about the situation either now or later, let it go, reminding yourself each time it comes back that you've already allocated it to the "cannot control" bin. And then refuse it any more headspace.

end

I TRUST I'VE MADE a convincing case throughout this book that as technology continues to create ever more customizable bubbles for us, despite all of the wonder that entails, it comes at a price.

Patience wanes.

Empathy—the ability to see, appreciate and value a point of view other than our own—erodes.

The willingness and, in a very real sense, even the *wherewithal* to reach happy compromise is lost.

And yet these connection points with the others around us aren't the only things to suffer. Perhaps one of the saddest and most insidious effects of having virtually everything at our fingertips is the mounting unwillingness *to let go.*

It used to be that when your grade-school friend moved cross country, you cried and exchanged addresses and promised to write. There were no cell phones, and for all but the wealthy, long-distance rates made anything other than holiday or emergency calls rare. And so you'd exchange letters from afar for a while. But after a few months, the frequency would wane. And after a year or so, your friend would remain mostly within the storybook of your memories.

When high school ended, you signed one another's yearbooks. You cheered shoulder to shoulder at homecoming and danced your heart out at senior prom, commenting aloud at every turn how whatever you were doing would be "the last time together." You had sleepovers where you stayed up all night and watched a movie you'd all seen a dozen times before, and reminisced and shed your tears. You marched to *Pomp and Circumstance* and threw your caps and felt that strange mix of exhilaration, trepidation and nostalgia. You hugged tightly and said your farewells and wished one another the best. Then, with few exceptions, you all moved on to the next chapter of your life.

Not so anymore.

People have social media accounts with a total number of connections ranging from hundreds on the low end— to hundreds of thousands, or even millions—allowing us to be found by and perpetually tied to even the most peripheral of acquaintances from all the way back to preschool. Every classmate. Every teacher. Every neighbor and babysitter. Every friend-of-a-friend you met once at that wedding.

Yet studies about the human capacity to maintain relationships (cf. Robin Dunbar, Oxford) show that, even at the outermost limit, we just aren't capable of maintaining more than 150 relationships in real life. And when we rule out all but close friends—those we'd physically call on in a crisis, let's say—the number drops starkly to just four or five.

What this means, in effect, is that we are caught in a loop of attempting to do the impossible.

We're continually depleting our limited resources of time and energy that, once upon a time, would have been invested into strengthening our bonds with that small handful of carefully chosen, inner-circle friends.

And so, ironically, in holding onto *everyone*, we fail to develop intimate relationships with *anyone*. We wind up with *more*—and yet so much less of what matters, what our souls actually crave.

If this were the extent of the problem, it would be bad enough. But it doesn't end there.

Not so very long ago, crow's feet and laugh lines were markers of a life well lived, graying hair an emblem of wisdom gained. Icons of stage and screen—Bette Davis, Katharine Hepburn, Humphrey Bogart—grew older right alongside us, wrinkles and all. And together, we aged as gracefully as we could.

That is, on the whole, we were better at letting go of our youth and embracing each stage of life as it came, without stigma.

But consider: how many times in the last week alone have you seen headlines, clickbait lists or social media posts scrutinizing, ridiculing and offering the most unflattering images of an aging star? "What happened to so-and-so? She used to be so hot, but look at her *now*!"

For crying out loud—*yes*, fifty years ago, she looked younger than she does now at 73.

And so those who can afford it try to hold onto a semblance of youth and avoid the criticism by undergoing painful and invasive surgeries. Sometimes, the procedures go horribly wrong, which of course only garners more public derision. But *sometimes*, they go right, delivering plumper lips, smoother brows, firmer jawlines.

And we watch through our glass-house windows the whole time, our minds filled with what we could—what we *should*—look like at 40 and 50 and 75. Ten thousand mirrors all imploring us to cling to youth by any means possible... *or else.*

And that's all to say nothing of the ongoing stream of digitally altered photos of seeming perfection being posted by our college roommate or the co-worker from that job we had back in '95.

Even our entertainment tastes reveal our reluctance to let go. In times gone by, most books and movies had a clear beginning, middle and ending. Sure, there have long been soaps and serials. But it's the new norm for us as media consumers to have worlds created for us to inhabit indefinitely through unending sequels and reboots and cinematic universes where plot is secondary and our heroes never die.

In short, we're more reluctant and ill-equipped than ever before to say goodbye.

TRIED

All good things must come to an end.

If you've read this book from the beginning, you'll recall our friend Geoffrey Chaucer, who cautioned us about throwing stones at houses (or heads) of glass. As it turns out, those weren't the only worthy words he bestowed upon the world.

In fact, even in a work as compact as this book, he's getting an encore in this the closing chapter. What's more, this final adage comes to us from the very same story from Chaucer: *Troilus and Criseyde.*

The original wording under present consideration was "**euery thyng hath ende**." No, those aren't typos. Remember, this was written about 650 years ago, back when spellings were quite different from now. But I'm confident you'll have had no trouble figuring it out.

If you're paying close attention, you will also have noticed the omission of an important word: *good*. And that would seem to significantly change the sentiment.

Chaucer's *Troilus and Criseyde* is broken into five "books" or acts, which modern translations list this way:

> **Book I**—Troilus's Love
> **Book II**—Love Encouraged
> **Book III**—The Consummation
> **Book IV**—The Separation
> **Book V**—The Betrayal

Our chapter's maxim is found smack dab in the middle: "The Consummation."

Getting more specific, our love-struck protagonist has just had the best night of his life rollicking with the fair Criseyde. At the end of the party, with Troilus all starry-eyed and sighing, the narrator basically says, "Eventually, since *everything ends sometime*, she had to leave." And so it's abundantly clear from the context that what was ending was, indeed, *good*.

However, it doesn't take more than a glance at the subtitles of the final two acts of the poem to understand that good things coming to an end had broader meaning.

...&...

It doesn't matter who you are, what your income or nationality or religion or orientation may be, one thing you hold in common with every other person on the planet is *endings*.

Endings don't discriminate.

Endings come in all sizes. Some we plan for and mark on our calendars. Others come unexpectedly. Our favorite fashions go out of style and go-to products are discontinued. New cars get dinged, begin to rust and finally give out completely. From summer camp to college, vacations to lifelong careers, teenage flings to sixty-year marriages— endings are just a part of life.

One of the best pieces of advice I've encountered on this topic comes by way of a Zen master. Ajahn Chah holds up a glass of water before his young student, saying (paraphrased):

> *Do you see this glass? I love this glass. It holds the water admirably. When I tap it, it has a lovely ring. When the sun shines on it, it reflects the light beautifully. But when the wind blows and the glass falls off the shelf and breaks, or if my elbow hits it and it falls to the ground, I simply say, "Of course!" When I know that the glass is already broken, every minute with it is precious.*

Some of you may close yourself off from this, for no other reason than learning that it comes from Zen teachings. You may believe it to be contrary to your own religion somehow. Or perhaps you will think that you are hardly the type of person who's capable of grasping and practicing anything so deep or philosophical. But where truth is found, it has existed before anyone put it to words. Likewise, truth inherently works when put into practice. This being the case, it matters very little whether truth comes by way of Mother Teresa or Mickey Mouse. So I encourage you to keep an open mind as we continue to consider this broken-glass mentality in light of the endings each of us inevitably faces.

(Still) **TRUE**

Since as far back as I can remember, I've been especially sensitive to both beginnings and endings. And summer time for me has always had a way of symbolizing both.

Every year when I was a kid, we would rent a house on Cape Cod for vacation. Crossing the Bourne or Sagamore Bridge, or even waiting in the car for my parents to retrieve the key from the rental agency, felt like a hold-your-breath beginning.

Time went slowly in the best of ways during those weeks. I would devour a stack of books while sitting in a low chair, my toes digging into the wet sand as the tide edged up or back, necessitating a move every so often to be sure my feet were occasionally splashed. Outdoor showers were the norm. Extended family clam boils with corn on the cob seemed to last and last. Naps were frequent. There was no sense of urgency, no thinking about the next day while the current day was in progress.

But eventually, and seemingly all at once, that last day would come. And *that* day always went by quickly. Whatever book I'd been reading ceased to hold any interest. Or perhaps I just lost focus. The sky looked different. There was even a change to the air. I could swear I smelled fall and school coming. And much too soon, one of the adults would announce that we'd better head back from the beach to the cottage. There'd be a lump in my throat as I brushed off my feet with a towel in the parking lot before getting in the car, purposefully not doing too good a job, so that I could keep that sand with me if only just a little longer.

I never slept well that final night in our vacation cottage. I thought. I reflected. Silent tears would spill over the corner of an eye into a pillow that had come to feel like a summer-camp friend.

Early on the morning of our departure, I would clip a piece of rug from some unseen corner or peel a fleck of paint from inside a closet in my room. It didn't much matter what it was, as long as it was part of the house. And I would carefully place these things into a small baggie or container along with a small slip of paper containing the address and the dates we'd stayed there. Once home again, it was days before I could put that keepsake away, leaving it by the bedside and looking at it until I fell asleep each night.

In this way, I am much the same as an adult. And given that this is regarding events as relatively minor as a vacation, it shouldn't be too difficult to imagine how deeply I internalize more significant endings such as broken relationships. Or death.

However, as someone who firmly believes that both

misery and happiness are *choices*—someone who puts this truth to the test daily—I've learned a thing or two about how to experience endings fully while not losing my anchor of peace and joy.

For instance, I've long held that regret is an utterly wasted emotion. And yet, while we may associate regret with the end of a thing, it is actually the result of choices we make *in the middle*, long before the "glass" of a thing breaks. In fact, it's that perpetual awareness of the already broken glasses in our lives that *allows* us to experience events and people in ways that never allow regret to take root.

You see, our saying for this final chapter isn't solely that "things must come to an end." It's equally about the *good things* that happen as part of the story. So before we continue with how to handle our endings, let's talk about creating and maximizing the *good things* that make up our middles.

Simply put, we do that by learning how to be *fully present.*

Now, I'm aware that the concept of being "fully present"—even the words themselves—may sound high-minded and transcendental to some (or as my close friends would say, "woo-woo").

To others, it will sound quite the opposite—cliché and trendy, a mere pop catchphrase for the self-help crowd.

For still others, it will evoke sensory images of plinky massage-parlor music, or a smiling Buddhist monk walking silently by a Koi pond while the echo of some distant gong reverberates in the distance.

I'd simply like to tell you what it means *to me*. My hope

is that, in doing so, it might also help you to decide what, if anything, it might mean to *you*. And due to the nature of the topic at hand and because I believe it will be of the most benefit, I'm going to chance breaking the fourth wall here for a bit and speak in the present tense.

Time passes in the same way here as when I was a kid during summer vacations, every day somehow feeling stretched into three or four.

Meanwhile, I've also had recent discussions with friends who have expressed that life feels as if it is blazing by, and all the faster as they get older. I can't help but notice that these same friends speak in equal proportion about feeling like they are always racing, distracted or frantic about future decisions or worries, perpetually tired, and never able to do the things that refill them or give them real joy.

Spending time with their kids.

Cooking in rather than ordering out or eating in the car while whizzing between unmemorable heres and theres.

Fostering their creative side.

Baking cookies for a friend.

However, the fact is that time is moving along at a constant rate for each of us—from that kid on summer vacation, to me during my wonderful and carefree stay in Florida, to those who feel as if their clocks are ticking away triple-time. So what is the difference?

The difference doesn't seem to be about having enough money. Kids don't have money. But they seem to have figured out how to slow down time.

It also doesn't appear to be based on how many orbits a person has completed around our central star. I know some sage old souls for whom time seems to be passing at quite a leisurely pace, much as it did for them during those summers eight decades ago.

So maybe it's work that's the trouble. Kids don't work, nor do the elderly. I'm not working (much) during my vacation. And yet, I honestly do know people who work the same number of hours as everyone else—sometimes more—and yet who have no complaint about the rate at which time is passing.

Simple logic would seem to say that if time is constant, any discrepancies in the passage of time are wholly *perceptual*. And if it is a matter of perception, then the possibility lies within each of us to alter that perception, which means that, by and large, it comes down to one thing…

Choice.

I myself will testify that, while I've most definitely been caught in "time traps" where weeks or months have seemed to blur by at head-spinning speed, I've also learned to live in such a way during "regular life" that moments tick and tock gently like that old Kit-Cat clock, its eyes and tail wandering lazily back and forth, smiling all the while.

Here's the conclusion I've come to.

Regardless of how you feel, you are in *the now*. That is, you exist in the present (and for all of my philosophical and religious friends, I'm begging you just this once to revert to your childlike selves and resist debating this assertion).

At the time you are reading this, you are where you are. You are nowhere else. You are no-*when* else. You are living this moment…

…and this one…

…at the same time and speed at which every other person on the planet is living it. The sense of unrest begins to rear its head when we try to jump through space and time to be two places or times at once. Or three. Or ten.

Then there are some of us whose days and nights are taken up more and more with looking through old photographs of when we were young, reminiscing about the "good old days"—   to the point where the ghosts of our past are stealing more of our attention than the living people and potential experiences that exist in the present. That is, we are trying to relive *beginnings* and *middles* at the same time.

Thing is, we're just not designed to be multiple places or times simultaneously. And so, in attempting to do the impossible, it stands to reason that we stress our system. We overload it. Steam builds up. Gears grind. It gets wonky. And before you know it—*SPROING!*—our perception of time is all out of whack.

You see, when I report that I am "frantic," what I mean is that I am attempting to send my mind ahead of me to "where else I should be" at this moment or "how much time is left" before I have to do X, rather than allowing my mind to join my body *where it is*.

And that is right here.

Right now.

When I allow myself to be overwhelmed with busyness (and that *is* a choice), I am attempting to control that uncontrollable space-time thingy by trying to stretch one hour to fit the activity that would require two.

When I nurse resentment, anger and regret, I'm yet again seeking to send my mind away from my body to somehow revisit decisions and hurts long past. I'm making the choice to burn up my mental machinery in vain attempts to rewrite history. Or I haunt old memories like a petulant poltergeist, looking on like Scrooge at phantoms of my own creation who are not aware of—nor interested in—my lingering presence there. Before I know it, the hands on the wall clock have once more inexplicably jumped hours ahead.

Being fully present is possible for *anyone*, not just for the modern-day Thoreau with the luxury to stroll his days away beside Walden Pond. It requires no climb to Machu Picchu. It costs nothing. And it is by no means "woo-woo."

It's a simple choice.

Notice that I said *simple*—not necessarily *easy*. It takes practice. It takes discipline. It takes consistency. But it is totally obtainable. And, if you ask me, it is totally worth it.

Here's how I stay fully present.

First, I try always to be mindful and intentional about letting go of bitterness and regret. Just as we don't want to jump forward to *endings* sooner than they arrive, we don't want to be jumping *backward* in our story, either.

Like bitterness and regret, worry is also a notorious time waster. There is a vast difference between wisdom and worry. One leads to outcome-changing planning and action, while the other leads only to more worry. The chasm is equally wide between reflection and regret. Whenever the past or the future begins to produce *anxiety*, it is working against you and not for you.

Next, in order to remain fully present, I try to be diligent in regularly asking myself "check-in" questions like these:

What have I taken on that I need to consider dropping?

Where am I squandering my emotional energy on the ineffectual neediness of others, or on petty things I need to release?

What decision could I make right now to restore a sense of peace and balance?

I'm not kidding. I really do ask myself these things. Then I clear some space for stillness, so that I can hear my own honest answers with clarity.

When I know what needs to change, I remind myself of the central truth in everything I write:

"You *always* have a choice."

I also remind myself that, if I were to suddenly die tomorrow, all the things I thought I needed to be doing— would still get done.

Or they wouldn't.

But one thing is certain: the world would keep right on turning without my having done them.

This humbling realization works wonders in helping me to see that I really can cut things from my life—or say no to other things looming overhead like a storm cloud. Might that upset some people or make for some awkward moments? Sure. Will it matter in a year? Or even a week? Most likely not. And if it did, that would be a choice on the part of *others*, not me. I can only control my own choices and reactions—no one else's.

Then, there are times when nothing particular is urgently pulling at me, but I still find myself woozy with that feeling that I'm somehow slipping from the present to… *some-when else.*

If I'm being honest, that has happened a few times as I've entered the second half of my wonderful vacation time here. I've found my mind trying to wander outside my "now"—counting how many (or few) days I have left, thinking about tasks that await back home, from something as seemingly trivial as wading through weeks of mail, to bigger undertakings like extensive client projects I know people are champing at the bit for me to complete for them.

But the reality of *this moment* is that I am *here*. I am *now*. And today is wonderful. It's got all the potential in the world to be one of those "good things" before these 24 hours ever come to an end. And so the last few days of my vacation, for all intents and purposes, are exactly the same as the day I arrived. *This* "today" is full of moments and possibilities, adventures of my own choosing. And tomorrow, when it arrives, will hold the same potential.

I'll leave you with one last thought before we move on: a mental exercise I often use to stay in the present and keep that perception of the passage of time in alignment with reality. Here's what I do whenever the feeling of "good things coming to an end" too soon encroaches on my "now." I put words to the present, whatever shape that is taking at the moment. I call this strategy "*I Am Here*."

For example, I'll actually say to myself something like this:

> *I am here*. *I am in this oversized chair right now. I have a big comfy pillow propped up behind my back and another across my lap. I am on page 537 of a book I'm really enjoying. I am wondering how this character will get out of his current predicament. I am chewing on a delicious cherry I took from the bowlful beside me. I'm enjoying myself right now. I am living this beautiful moment.* **I am here**.

It's very important that you only put into words what is true at this moment, and that you don't include what *isn't happening*. For instance, adding in "*My bills are not due right now*" defeats the purpose. I'm sure you can guess where the focus would immediately shift.

For you, it may sound like this:

> *I am here*. *I am driving. My hands are comfortably around the steering wheel. I can hear and feel the road passing underneath. I can smell the vanilla air freshener. I'm taking a deep breath and feeling it go out.* **I am here**.

Above all, focus on the positive.

I challenge you to put it to the test, to experience once again what time felt like for that summertime you of yesteryear: listening from your tree house as the breeze rustled the leaves; or being suspended on air as your swing reached its full height, the exhilaration of it tickling your stomach as you began another descent.

Let me be clear: I don't have this down pat. There

are times when I catch myself missing "good things" in present moments for the sake of trying to control future ones. And there are days when I have to revisit my "*I Am Here*" dialogue twenty times to make it through. But as I continue to practice being fully present, that misperception that time is racing by happens far less often than it used to.

Time is neither your enemy nor your friend. Time simply *is*. What you *do* with it is a matter of *choice*.

~~*Not*~~ **TRUE**

We've now considered some ways to delay life's endings by learning to be fully present during our "middles." Yet, as this final piece of **tried-and-(still)-true** advice reminds us, "All good things *must come to an end*."

I debated whether what follows should continue under this (*Still*) **TRUE** subheading, or whether it should pick up in the final **Not** TRUE section. I found it more challenging than in previous chapters to clearly explore happy, healthy approaches without delving into the not-so-helpful alternatives we often fall into. In other words, it's been tougher to say "do this" without implying "…which means stop doing that."

After a bit of consideration, I decided that where the section breaks occur is not all that important. What *is* important as we work our way to the ending of this chapter—and this book—is that you look at each choice to let go of negative mindsets and habits as a simultaneous choice to make room for positive ones.

Acknowledging that "all good things must come to an

end" is not a cause for despair. It is not a justification to mope around the edges of life with Eeyore-like pessimism, refusing to invest in anyone or anything and citing the perpetual mantra, "Why bother? It won't last anyway."

No, a true understanding of the glass already being broken doesn't lead to avoiding glasses. Quite to the contrary, it provides a continual reason to celebrate—to more deeply experience and appreciate—those many good things in our lives, because we know our time with each is limited and therefore something to be treasured.

I've reminisced quite a bit in this final chapter about vacations past, how each one has represented both "good things" and "an end." At first, I wondered if some readers might not be able to bridge the connection between the relatively light and admittedly temporary endings associated with vacations, and the heavier real-life endings some may be facing: closing chapters on childhood and youth, declining health, break-ups, divorce, empty nests, retirement, aging parents—deaths. Please know that I myself have not been immune from these and have experienced most.

Upon further consideration, however, I decided to keep the vacation imagery for a number of reasons. While it is all true, I hope that it will serve as a gentle allegory of sorts for the many deeper things we each must let go of along the way. I've just found that, where time allows, providing a safe *and gradual* way for people to address their areas of pain accomplishes more than putting a finger directly on a wound. And storytelling can create that bit of distance, a place from which we can see the terrain of our own lives more clearly.

That said, let me return to the end of a vacation, trusting you to apply the analogy to the endings in your own life.

The night before my trip to a beautiful vacation home to Florida, I had gone out and bought one of those giant pill organizers for people who have to take meds four times per day. It had 28 little snap compartments, all of which I clicked open once I got home. I grabbed my thyroid medication and systematically dropped one pill into each of the partitions. Then I grabbed a handful of my daily multivitamin and added those, one by one: *plink, plink, plink.* Next was my Super B-Complex, then the supplemental D3, and on it went. It took a long time, but I got into the rhythm of it and didn't mind in the least.

When I was done, I called my best friend. "Wow! I'm looking at all the pills I'll have to take while I'm away," I chimed, "and it's making me realize—I'm going to be gone for a nice long time!" We both snorted with sudden laughter at my unlikely "hourglass" and how fitting a marker it was of yet another birthday around the corner, which I'd celebrate soon, there in Florida. I mean, when you start merrily marking the length of a vacation in pills, let's face it—*you're old.*

The next morning, I was off.

I remarked many times while away that a week seemed like a month, in the best of ways. But at some point during my time away, as I wandered into the kitchen to grab a tangy lime pop, I happened to peek down through the clear multi-color lids of the pill organizer and notice that more were empty than full.

It's silly, but this small moment was significant to me.

Then there was the day I could definitively count the

scant number of filled compartments at a glance. Suddenly, there was a catch in my throat, and a prickly pressure built at the front of my eyes.

It's almost over.

The time had come to put into practice those "I am here" strategies I shared with you earlier, in order to stay fully present: to enjoy this moment and not let thoughts of future or past moments rob me of *now*.

As the pills continued to dwindle, I found myself having those inner "I am here" dialogues more frequently until, inevitably, that last 24 hours arrived. My dialogues began to change slightly, to include things like these:

This is the last time for this year that I'll wash this dish.

This is the last time I'll sleep in this bed, on these pillows.

Well, this is the last tangy lime pop.

Like I said, nestling into those "last time" pillows feels different somehow, like saying goodbye to the friends you made during summer camp. Gathering the sheets for the last loads of laundry—even putting the box to the lime pops into the recycling bin and closing the lid—it's sentimental to me. I don't burst into tears, but I *do* feel the sting of them.

Truth be told, occasionally one will spill over.

And I let it.

As I mentioned, I've really always been this way, as far back as I can remember. And while I am all for continued personal growth, this is *not* an area of myself I ever want to change.

end

The time was drawing nearer. The laundry was all done. The beds had all been made to perfection, with great care not only to leave them neat and tidy, but to give that extra fluff to each pillow so that it would be all the more inviting to whomever might arrive next to start their own magical escape.

With the Florida sunshine streaming in, I sat in the high-backed leather chair and wrote my entry in the Guest Book, smiling and sniffling the whole time (being careful not to drip on the pages). Then I made the rounds, closing each of the blinds, slowly, one by one.

With the house now in shadow, I ambled out into the front lanai and dipped my feet in the pool for a few moments, kicking them back and forth like a kid.

I breathed deeply. *I am here*, I told myself. If even for just a few more moments—*I am here*.

Finally, and a bit reluctantly, I pulled my feet from the water and walked back inside barefoot. I closed and locked the lanai door, which seemed somehow to click too loudly.

I threw my backpack over a shoulder and rolled my bag down the tiled hallway to the door, turning back one last time in the darkness and silence to say goodbye.

And *thank you*.

I closed the garage door, then loaded my things into my friend's waiting vehicle, hopped into the passenger seat (with my sunglasses on for more reasons than sun) and pulled out of the driveway, looking back through the window as long as I could, until no part of the house or yard was any longer visible.

Why am I writing about all of this? What's my point? Just to indulge myself? Or to see if I can get you other softies like me to cry a little?

Nope.

"But what about choosing happiness rather than falling into the trap of letting thoughts of the future or the past encroach on the joy of the present moment?" you may be asking. "How do sentimentality and tears fit in with staying present?" Some of you might even be arguing, "Aren't these feelings brought on, in essence, by *reluctance to let go of past moments* or to enter the inevitability of a 'new present'?"

I suppose, for some, that might be true. For me, however, it's actually *part* of my being fully present.

You see, to deny the tears in such moments would be trying to move prematurely into a future that has not yet arrived—even if that future will arrive in mere minutes.

I recently became acquainted with this quote:

> **Don't cry because it's over;**
> **smile because it happened.**

I see why people like it. But I think you have to look beyond the surface meaning of the words to see the wisdom held here. And it seems to me that this is about *living* in the past—in a perpetual state of wistfulness or melancholy or regret—and not about denying ourselves the *full experience of present emotion*.

Perhaps a better expression is this one, brought to us by Dr. Seuss:

> **Be who you are and say what you feel,**
> **because those who mind don't matter**
> **and those who matter don't mind.**

Being who I am means fully feeling what I feel in the present moment. And truly, what I feel in those moments of sentimentality isn't exactly what I'd call *sadness*, and certainly not despair. As I witnessed many times during that wonderful time away, rain showers and storms sometimes come even as the sun is shining brightly between the clouds all the while. What I feel at those times of letting go is something more like that.

Staying mindful that each glass is already broken doesn't mean we feel nothing when "that day" finally comes and it breaks. Rather, it means that we embrace our fortunate present with the glass, all the while living at peace with the knowledge that, someday, we will need to feel the loss of it and perhaps to let some tears fall.

Yet an integral part of that mindfulness is always, "…and then I will sweep up the shards and I will move on."

The pain of a loss is directly proportional to the amount we were willing to invest along the way, a tribute of sorts. And let me say plainly that there is no set timeline for moving through grief. The important thing is that we are, indeed, *moving*. And it's harder to find that forward momentum if the first time we've ever considered that every glass breaks—*is the moment it breaks*.

I repeat, however, that a healthy perspective doesn't lead to glum and withdrawn living.

We don't start dating someone or get married and think, "This will probably end in bitter flames." Rather, we acknowledge what will always be true of every beginning— that one day, however distant, there is a letting go. Even the wedding vows spoken by most on one of the happiest days of their life includes "…till death do us part." And yet we feel *joy* while speaking or hearing these words. There is nothing morose about that vow. It is a simple and powerful agreement we make: *I will love and cherish 'us' every day until this glass breaks.*

In the same way, an expecting mother doesn't detach from the process simply because of the knowledge that this baby will eventually grow up, move away and have a life independently of her. We take pictures of that first birthday party, not ignorant of the fact that an 18th birthday lies somewhere ahead. We make videos of first words and first steps, realizing full well that not every word spoken during the teenage years may be a cause for joy, not every step placed on the path we might hope. And our response *should* be to celebrate those many good things our precious little ones do—not *despite* the endings we know will someday come, but *because* of them. A healthy awareness of those future endings continually reminds us:

Be present.

Be patient.

Drink this in.

Laugh aloud and often.

Speak the love you're feeling.

Make much of little moments.

Because each is a diamond facet of *right now* that will never sparkle quite the same way again.

And that is true of *every* "right now"…

…including this one.

end

With that, your reading of *Tried & (Still) True*—which I very much hope has been a "good thing"—comes to its own end. As is the nature of things, even if you read it again, *this* experience as it has been can never be repeated, but rather will mark another new and unique beginning.

What it *becomes* from here however, by way of choice and change, is entirely up to you.

Questions & A Challenge

1. How well do you do living in the present moment? Which culprits most often pull you from living fully in the present: regret, worry, resentment, nostalgia for times past, fear of the future, busyness or others?

2. Is it (or has it typically been) hard for you to let "good things comes to an end" in a way that feels healthy to you? What types of "good things" are hardest for you to let go when they end?

3. What is your response to the Zen teaching of seeing every glass in life as "already broken"? What are some areas where this teaching might help you appreciate and embrace the present while being better prepared for the future?

CHALLENGE: Over the next week, practice the "I Am Here" strategy as much as possible. Pause what you are doing, breathe and focus on the good things about your present surroundings or circumstances. At the close of each day, jot down a short description of the places, times and circumstances when you applied the strategy throughout the day (e.g., when I was feeling hurried during breakfast; after meeting with my first client; during lunch when I started thinking about my upcoming test, etc.). For the sake of this challenge, try setting a specific goal for the number of times you'll practice the strategy before considering the challenge met, perhaps 25 times. When the challenge has been completed, reflect on how this experiment worked for you. Is it something you might put in your "toolbox" moving forward? Did it give you other ideas for ways to stay present?

One Final Challenge
& Personal Request from Erik

Now that you've completed the book, I have a simple request of you: would you leave a review of *TRIED & (Still) TRUE* on Amazon?

Your review will directly impact the reach that this book is able to have. Reviews are often the number one reason shoppers will choose a book or pass it by.

And I read each and every review myself; so your review would be a personal encouragement to me as I continue to mentor, write, speak and do all I can to spread positivity, purpose and hope to others.

If you are willing to do that for me, I've created a simple, step-by-step guide to writing your Amazon review. It takes all the stress and guesswork out of it. You can download that guide from my website using the link below:

tinyurl.com/TriedTrueReview

And if you're already a pro at leaving book reviews, simply log into your Amazon account now to share your opinion.

Thank you!

about the author

ERIK TYLER

Erik is an author, speaker, blogger, mentor, facilitator, people-lover, creative force, conversationalist, problem solver, chance-taker, noticer and lover of life. He lives in the Boston area.

facebook.com/eriktylerauthor
@BestAdviceSoFar
booking@TheBestAdviceSoFar.com
www.TheBestAdviceSoFar.com

If you enjoyed **TRIED & (STILL) TRUE**, check out
Erik Tyler's first book, **The Best Advice So Far**.
Start reading *right now* with BONUS material
including more than three full chapters!

The Best Advice
So Far

EXCERPTS

BONUS

**Courage is doing
what you're afraid to do.
There can be no courage
unless you're scared.**

*Eddie Rickenbacker, WWI flying ace
and Medal of Honor recipient*

CHAPTER 1

Choice

W HAT I AM ABOUT TO SAY is foundational to all that will follow in this book. Don't race through it. Spend some time with it. Read it several times if you must. If you can really internalize it and live it, it could quite literally change your life.

First, as is my way, I'd like to start with a story.

I mentor teens. I've done so for more than two decades. By mentor, I do not mean that I've joined an organization and agreed to spend a block of time each week with a teen. While I certainly encourage and see the value in this type of commitment, my mentoring takes a broader scope. At any given time, I'm investing in twelve to twenty young people on a personal, day-to-day basis.

A couple of years back, I had about a dozen seniors I was mentoring. We'd sort of formed a band of brothers back when they were freshmen. It was now April, and many of the guys were suddenly and simultaneously falling apart. Frantic calls at all hours. Lengthy, erratic emails. One of them had even asked to come over near midnight. When he arrived, he sat on my couch shaking and in tears, trying to explain that he had been having repetitive nightmares and was generally panicked at all times. I listened as he gushed for a while. Then I looked at him sagaciously. "I see.

I think I know exactly what's going on." His eyes widened, as if he were sure I would tell him the term for some rare form of psychosis, which he would readily have believed he had.

"*What is it?*" he pleaded, tears still falling.

"You're graduating," I replied, smiling.

In addition to hanging out one-on-one or in smaller clusters during the week, this entire group of guys met together on Mondays at my place for dinner and open dialogue. That particular week's discussion point was a given. I've always thought it negligent somehow that society doesn't better prepare seniors for this phenomenon: the emotional upheaval that accompanies stumbling headlong from childhood into adulthood. It seems as obvious and necessary a topic as the birds and the bees. The simple fact, I told them, is that sometime during the three months before or after graduation, when faced with the end of life as they know it and the beginning of life as they *do not* know it—high school seniors have a period of what feels a lot like mental breakdown. They wander through an unpredictable maze of fear, lethargy, mania and other erratic moods. I told them that, as odd and scary as it may feel, this was completely normal. And that set their minds at ease that they weren't, in fact, going crazy like Great Aunt Bertha.

As we went around the circle, pressed in close along the olive sectional in my living room, each of them shared how they had been feeling, relieved to hear that they weren't the only one. Until we got to Chad.

Chad was different. He was charisma incarnate. And while he listened attentively to the others, offering encouragement and good advice, when it came to his turn, he just couldn't relate. "Gee," he said, all smiles, "I just don't feel *any* of that. And I can't imagine why I ever *would!* I'm excited about college. I'm comfortable with new people and situations. I can't wait to graduate and get started!"

I didn't want to dull his shine. And, if anyone were of the constitution to escape senior panic, it was Chad. But I did want him to be prepared, should it creep up on him later. "That's terrific!" I said. "Just keep it tucked away, in case it hits later on." He shrugged and let it go with a noncommittal "OK."

Graduation came and went. Chad was bubbling over with enthusiasm. He even staged an ostentatious stumble and trip across the lawn as he went to receive his diploma, eliciting a few colorful but good natured words from the principal, who apparently forgot his microphone was on. Chad's graduation party was the hit of the summer. True to his prediction, he remained deliriously optimistic and excited about heading off to college, where he would follow in his father's footsteps, having enrolled as a pre-med student.

I helped him pack the day he headed off. I actually think it was a far tougher day for me than it was for him. I stood in the driveway as the family drove away, Chad waving from the window like a lunatic and shouting back, "I love you, Papa!" (one of his many nicknames for me).

A few days later, I was out having lunch with a friend when a text came through. It was Chad:

Really not doing so hot.
Need to talk.
Call if you can.

I excused myself and called immediately. The voice that answered was barely recognizable. Chad was hoarse and sobbing. Hard.

"Tell me what's going on," I invited.

Chad stumbled over his words, choking through the torrent of tears. Everyone he'd encountered at college was "fake," he told me. No one thought he was funny there. He was on a campus of thousands and felt completely alone. His professor for calculus was Bulgarian. He couldn't understand her, other than that she had made it clear that she really didn't want to be teaching this class but had been made to by the higher-ups. He was presently curled up in fetal position on his bed in a dark dorm room, finding it unimaginable that he could get up and go to the next class, let alone continue for the long haul at this desolate campus. His world was crumbling. His dreams were over.

It was the first week of classes.

I welled up as he let it all drain out of him. It would have been pitiful had it been anyone, but being Chad—perpetually cheerful Chad—it was all the more heart-wrenching.

"OK, Chad," I said when his words had run out, "remember that conversation we had about the panic that hits everyone? It's hitting you. It's normal. You just hit yours a few days late. It will pass. I promise."

Whimpers on the other end of the line.

"Second, you need to go and drop this calculus class

today. It's your first semester. Four classes is fine. You'll feel so much better."

Chad sniffed. "Really?" Something like hope was breaking through. "I can just *do* that?"

"Yes, Chad, you can do that," I said with gentle authority. "You can drop or change every class if you want, and it's still early enough that you won't be charged a cent to do it."

"Yeah, then I'm going to do that. I just didn't know I could. That will be great."

As we talked about Chad's other classes, it seemed he wasn't thrilled with many, even those not being taught by less-than-willing Bulgarians.

Finally, I asked the pivotal question. "Chad... *why* did you choose pre-med?"

He paused. "I don't know," he finally replied. "I guess— my dad and I just always talked about me being a doctor like him, and I guess that seemed fine to me. I couldn't think of anything else I wanted to do, so I just went with that."

"I see. How would you feel about changing that major to something you will actually *enjoy*?"

Chad didn't say anything, but the sun may as well have been shining through the cell phone. "You know what?" he chirped. "*I hate pre-med! I hate science!*" We both laughed openly, even through our sniffling.

We decided that each of us would separately look through the handbook at all of the majors offered by the university. We'd circle anything that we thought was a better possibility, given Chad's personality and interests. The next day, we compared notes. Chad was ecstatic.

Every ounce of despair had been replaced with joy. Among a handful of others, we had both wound up double circling this long shot of an option, but one that just seemed so... *Chad*: Human Services/Rehabilitation.

It was settled. He was changing his major.

"I don't know what my dad will say," Chad chimed, "and I know that it won't pay anything close to a doctor's salary. But I'm *so excited* about it!" He clamored on about the great class lists and the cool professors and the opportunities available to students in this major.

As it turned out, Chad had a great talk with his father. His parents wound up being the biggest supporters of his new major. And, not only did Chad change his major, he began to change the entire campus. He founded a unique club of which he was the president, a club that continues to this day and whose mission is to take positive social risks. And both he and the club have garnered lots of notice. He was featured on the radio and in the newspapers. He met with high administrators who were eager to back his efforts, and even wound up catching the personal attention of the president of the university.

Nice story. But what does this have to do with you? Well, you see, even an ultra-optimist like Chad fell apart and was completely overwhelmed and despondent, because he'd forgotten a very important truth. He was immobilized, because he believed in that space of time that life was *happening to him*, and that he had no say in the matter. Yet, once he was reminded of this key truth, he not only rebounded but began to take the world by storm.

THE BEST ADVICE SO FAR:
You *always* have a choice.

Chad did not need to be a doctor. There was no rule that said he must struggle through a schedule of classes he hated, or even that he needed to remain at that university. Chad had choices.

If you don't accept this truth—that you always have a choice—if you don't remember it and *live it*, then you are left to play the part of the victim in life. You begin (or continue) to live as if life is happening to you, that you are powerless, oppressed by your circumstances. But, if you truly change your mindset to believe and live out in practical ways that, in every circumstance, you have a choice—now, you open a door for *change*. Instead of living as if life is happening to you, *you* will begin to happen to *life*. You will begin to realize the difference that one person—you—can make, that you are an agent of change in your own life and in the lives of others.

Don't misunderstand me. I'm not saying that we get to choose everything that happens to us in life. We do not choose abuse, for instance, and we can at no time choose to undo those things which have happened to us in life.

We do not choose illness. We do not choose when or how the people we love will leave us. Or die.

We *do*, however, have the choice of how we will *respond* in every situation, even the hurtful ones. Instead, so often, we pour our frustration and anger into those things we can not change, rather than investing that energy into the many choices that we *can* make from that point forward.

I saw this painted on a classroom wall recently:

HARDSHIP IS GUARANTEED.
MISERY IS OPTIONAL.

I devote a whole chapter to this concept later on in the book. But for now, let that sink in. In the worst of circumstances that life may bring, you always have the next move. You have a choice.

In grieving, will you choose to close yourself off from others? Or will you live with more passion and intention, realizing the precious nature of life?

Will you let the abuser rob you of continually more hours and days and years of your life, through bitterness and anger? Or will you take the steps to thrive and live in the now, using your experience to help others do the same?

So it is with any advice. It is always your choice to try it out. Or to discard it. You can skim the pages of this book, mentally assenting or theoretically debating with me about why such-and-such wouldn't actually work in real life. Or you can come along for the adventure, try some new things, and see what happens.

The choice is yours.

CHAPTER 2

Negativity

I KNOW SOME PEOPLE—too many of them, really—who seem to be in a perpetually bad mood. These people drift along, frequent sighs having replaced anything akin to wind in their sails. They have somehow managed to find the worst jobs with the meanest bosses and most backstabbing co-workers. Asking "How are you?" is met with a tragic roll of eyes and sucking of teeth. The quaver in the opening word of the reply—"Well..."—indicates that you will not escape any time soon, but will be subjected to a lengthy and painstaking tale of woe. It seems that whenever I run into one of these people, they have coincidentally just that morning had some streak of catastrophic bad luck or other. Despite their obviously tragic circumstances, they report that their unfeeling family and so-called friends continue to criticize, hurt and reject them. Traffic jams, illness and botched orders at the drive-through are attracted to these people like dirty cosmic magnets.

I feel bad for these people. But it is not because of some plight with which they've been cursed. I feel bad for them, because they have unnecessarily spent so many unhappy years with a continual knot in their stomach.

THE BEST ADVICE SO FAR:
Being miserable is a choice.

Some of you just got mad. My short piece of advice feels like judgment to you. You're telling yourself that I don't understand, that this is a generalization, that your circumstances are far more complex or a special case.

At least hear me out. Then you will have all of the information, even if it is only to better fuel your anger toward me in the end. Might as well make your fire a doozy.

Or maybe, it will be the unimaginable—happiness. Freedom. Peace. If you will at least entertain the possibility, then you've already chosen to put your foot in the door to a better place.

I recently saw a short video about a man named Nick. As the video begins, the camera is zoomed in on Nick's face. He is a young, handsome man with a cool Australian accent. (Then again, to Americans, an Australian accent is always cool.) His voice is warm and friendly. You instantly like Nick. You know somehow without a doubt that, whatever he may be about to say, he is not acting. Nick announces that he likes to swim, boat, play golf. It almost seems like a dating advertisement. After the short list, which manages to exclude "long walks on the beach," Nick finishes his greeting: "I love life. I—am happy."

The camera zooms out. Nick is on a couch. Nick has no arms. Or legs. Well, he has something there where a leg should be—one small misshapen appendage, which he later refers to as his "chicken wing."

Nick's list of things he loves to do quickly takes on new meaning from this angle. In a montage sequence, we see Nick on the grass in front of a soccer goal. A ball goes flying over his head into the net. "I wasn't ready!" he exclaims, with a feigned look of childlike excuse. Next, we watch as Nick runs—yes, runs without legs—down the field. He balances a soccer ball on his head far longer than I can. He sloshes down a waterslide. Surfs. Steers a motor boat with his chin. Dives into a swimming pool. Plays golf (again, far better than I can).

But the purpose of Nick's video is not to illustrate some one-in-a-billion scientific anomaly. There are no doctors' testimonials, saying, "We don't know why this man can do these things. It should be impossible given his condition." The purpose of Nick's video is to tell others that being miserable is a choice. And that, conversely, happiness is also a choice. Nick is an international motivational speaker who tells his story so that the very same advice I've given you here has a voice that's difficult to argue with.

But it's still the same advice. True is true.

Nick doesn't paint some Pollyanna picture of his life. We see aides having to pick him up and move him onto a stage or an interview chair. He talks openly about having tried to drown himself in a bathtub at the age of eight, because he saw his life having no possibility for happiness. He would never be married. No one would love him that way. He was a drain on his parents and society. Nick had every circumstantial reason to be miserable. And for a while, he was.

Understand that his circumstances didn't change. He did not get prosthetic limbs. He still needs help in the bathroom, I'm guessing. But something changed, that much is certain. He took the exact same circumstances he'd been handed and *decided*, "If I am going to live, I am not going to live like this." He did not get happier after learning to run or swim. He learned to run and swim, because he decided to start being happier. And happiness breeds hope. He has found a purpose for his life—successfully encouraging hundreds of thousands of people to believe that life is what you make it. That you can always get back up and try again.

Nick is not an isolated case. I know many such people. A friend of mine, Anindaya, has been deaf and blind since childhood. He was not born deaf and blind. He lost his hearing gradually, due to a degenerative condition. He lost the sight in each eye in separate, random accidents in his native country of India. Talk about grounds for bitterness! But he is one of the happiest people I have ever met. He travels the world, unaided except by his dog. He completed an advanced degree and holds a high-ranking teaching position. He is an inventor. He is probably the smartest person I know. And he is married and very much in love.

Maybe this is a good time to bring it back to you. If you've got the miserable bug bad, you probably read those stories and felt some negative emotion. How did *they* figure out how to be happy when I can't? I'm a terrible person. I'm selfish. So I guess I deserve the miserable life I have. And, man, am I miserable. Just this morning, I blew a tire…And off it goes down that path again.

I was just talking with my niece about a woman we both know. I commented to this mother about how impressed I was with her toddler's memory. "He's a bright one! He's sitting in there quoting the movie we watched last night, line for line!" In an Eeyore-like voice, she replied, "Yeah.

Great. That's because he's seen it a million times. He drives me crazy."

Now, is her two-year-old intelligent, exhibiting solid memory and language skills at an early age? Or is he obsessive and annoying?

My best friend Dib is famous for putting it this way: "The only prize for being the most miserable is ... [*deliver next lines with zealous enthusiasm and a gasp of delight*] 'CONGRATULATIONS! You're the Most Miserable!' [*applaud here, then extend invisible interview mic*] "Tell us—how does it feel? You must be *so proud!*"

The nub of it is that there is no gain to being miserable. You're just miserable.

I remember a story I heard once, about a young mother baking a ham. She cut substantial-sized portions off the end of the ham and set them aside. Then she basted the remaining center portion, dressed it, and placed it in the oven.

"Why do you cut the ends off?" her inquisitive six-year-old daughter asked.

The mother paused, then replied, "That's just the way we always did it!"

"But why?" pressed the little girl, expectantly.

"Run along and play," the mother replied. But she was bothered at her own lack of any real answer. Her family *had* always done it that way. She called her own mother.

"Mom, I'm baking a ham and I cut the ends off, as usual. But ... why *did* we always cut the ends off?"

There was a silence on the line, followed by, "I ... don't really know. We just always did it that way in my family."

The call ended there, but the burning question lingered. The young woman now called her grandmother.

"Hi, Grandma. I have an odd question. Why do we cut the ends off the ham before we put it in the oven?"

"Goodness me," replied her grandmother, "I can't imagine why *you* do it. I only did it because my oven was too small to fit a whole ham."

Consider this carefully. We do virtually nothing in life without some sort of perceived gain. A man trapped by a fallen boulder while climbing endures the horror of cutting his own arm off with a small knife, because he believes there is a gain. Survival. Likewise, we complain, focus on the negative, or respond with sarcasm because there is a perceived gain.

Understand that I said *perceived* gain. Like the young mother in the anecdote, we often get ourselves into situations where we have long since stopped asking what the gain is. However, if we were to spend some thoughtful time answering this question, we may be forced to realize that the end result we were after isn't being achieved. Maybe it has *never* been achieved. And that means we've simply been wasting a whole lot of precious energy that could have been expended in more productive ways.

Maybe for you, this answer to the question of gains will rise to the surface: "I want people to pay attention to me. I never got attention as a kid except for when I was very sick." And so somewhere along the way, sickness—and the collecting of other dire circumstances—became your only hope for being taken seriously and getting the attention a child craves. A helpful realization. But ask yourself, "Am I, in fact, getting more affirming attention from people with my complaining and negative outlook?" The answer is likely no. The answer is more likely that people actually avoid your company or don't often call looking to spend time with you. The intended goal is not being reached.

My aim in this particular book is not to give a case-by-case rundown of all psychological possibilities for what unachieved goals are driving each person's negative emotions and perceptions. It is only to say that there is ample support and research, not to mention countless testimonials, to say that circumstances are not the problem. Choices regarding focus and behavior are. And those can be changed, with diligence. And perhaps a little help from others. I add my own life to the testimonials, and I hope that some of the principles in this book will provide solid suggestions for change.

So where do you start? How do you change what may perhaps be a lifetime of feeling like a victim?

Old habits die hard. They won't change overnight. That much is sure. But they *can* change.

The first step would be to accept that you have become a negative person, and that life or other people are not to blame. This is also the start of embracing that you are part of the solution. Not quite convinced that your problem is all that serious? Ask the three people closest to you. Don't lead the witness, using phrasing like "You don't see me as a negative person, do you?" Ask neutrally. Border on begging for an honest response: "I need to ask you something. It's serious and I need you to tell me the truth. I will not argue with whatever your answer is, I just need to know what you think. Do you see me as a negative person?" Then just listen. Be aware that, from people who love you, the answers you get may be tempered: "What do you mean by negative?" or "I might say you're more serious than negative exactly." Take anything but "No, of course not!" as a "Yes, you tend to be negative."

Breathe. Here comes the hard part, that will bring you face to face with finding out what those perceived gains of yours are. *Tell the people in your life that you are committing to stop being negative. Miserable. Sarcastic. A complainer.* Tell the people to whom you complain most. Tell them that you are resolved not to dwell on negative things any longer, but to focus on the positive. Give them permission to call you out on it when you slip. If you really consider doing this, you may find yourself thinking things like, *I can't do that! If I tell them, I won't be able to _____ anymore.* What you fill into that blank is likely your perceived gain. *I won't be able to get my kids to do what I want them to do anymore. I won't be able to pass the blame for my own failures anymore. I won't have a reason for people to feel bad for me anymore, and that's the closest I feel to loved.*

But again, ask yourself, is your perceived goal being met by the negativity anyway? Likely not. The kids ignore you when you gripe and nag. Others aren't keeping you from the consequences of your shortcomings. Complaining doesn't leave you feeling loved.

So, commit to your new course of action, tell people, and then set a new goal. An achievable goal. Spend time with your kids. Make it your goal to listen to them and understand what's important to them. Make it your goal to gain new job-related or interpersonal skills. Make it your goal to spread cheer and hope to others. As soon as you realize you are getting negative—even if it is only in your mind—stop yourself and admit it. If you are in conversation, admit it out loud: "You know what? I just realized I'm complaining and focusing on the bad here. I'm really trying to be more positive. So, I'm not even going to finish that story."

Don't give in just because the other person offers that "you have to vent sometime" or "it's OK with a good friend like me." It isn't OK. Even if they are content to listen to it, complaining isn't helping *you* to achieve your goal of peaceful and happy living. It is just keeping the old cycle going—the cycle that you are now committed to breaking.

Understand here that being negative isn't an all-or-nothing state. I consider myself a very positive person, but I still have my things that pull me toward moping or complaining. Just the other day, I was running this chapter by my friend Chad, who is probably the most positive person I know. And still, we both were able to notice in one another areas or times when we give in to being negative. There is always room for growth, for redirecting wasted energies into more positive pursuits.

I'd also like to say that, like Nick, you may have legitimately difficult circumstances. But Nick realized at some point early on that what he wanted was arms and legs. A normal life. And it became clear to him that being sad and angry wasn't going to give him those things. So he changed his goal. He decided that, rather than pining for the "normal life" of those who have all their limbs, he would pursue a different goal. A life of *purpose*. *That* goal was achievable, with specific action. And having positive, achievable goals, paired with a specific plan of action to reach them, will change our outlook on life.

CHAPTER 3

Positivity

S O, YOU'VE LOOKED in the proverbial mirror and decided that you complain or become negative more than you'd like. You're committed to change. Great! But now what? When you feel that black bubble rising inside, do you stuff it back down by sheer will power? Do you just grin and bear it when things go awry? Is the goal simply not saying negative things and hoping it changes how you feel?

It is certainly true that misery loves company, in the sense that negativity only breeds more negativity. The more we speak negative words, the more we perceive the world and other people through a negative lens. It stands to reason (as well as research) that speaking fewer negative things causes our outlook on life to be less negative.

But that is not the end goal, to simply be "less negative." While living at dead center may trump living in a funk, the real goal is to learn to live more positively — to actually see the beauty and wonder that already exists in the people and circumstances around us.

THE BEST ADVICE SO FAR:
Practice positivity.

This does *not* mean "Buck up, camper!" or "You just need to pull yourself up by the bootstraps!" The goal is not to behave in a more positive or palatable manner outwardly. The goal is to actually *become* more positive on the inside.

No one who is great at anything became so by simply deciding to be great. Likewise, you cannot just decide to be more positive. It takes *practice*. And practice is work.

Every cloud has a silver lining. This may at first sound like some platitude that your great-grandmother might have doled out, back in the days when people borrowed cups of sugar from neighbors and thought clean humor was funny and didn't seem to know very much at all about how complicated the world really is. I'd like to challenge you to dust off this saying and to practice it. Practice it like an athlete practices in preparation for the Olympics. Write it on a sticky note and put it on your dashboard. Set your phone to send you a reminder midway through your day. Heck… frame it and hang it on your wall.

Sounds nice in theory. But how does it work in a real-world setting?

First, consider it a challenge. A contest. You win if you can find the positive side in each seemingly negative situation. (If it helps, you can keep track of your score on that sticky note that's on your dash.)

I'm going to tell you a story. I like stories. This story is true.

I woke up one morning this week and went to take a shower. When I turned on the water, it hissed and sputtered, glugging out a pathetic amount of water. Then it just dripped, emitting a high-pitched whine. I turned the lever off, fuming. *I pay for hot water, and now I'm going to be late for my ten o'clock appointment!* I picked up the phone and stabbed in the numbers for the property management office. When the office attendant answered, I tore into him.

"*Why* do I have no hot water?" I said ominously. "I have someplace to be in a half hour."

"I just got a notice on that, sir. Let me see . . ." He fumbled through some papers. "Yes, they're replacing your furnace today, sir. It shouldn't be more than two hours."

"*Two hours?* You have to be kidding me!" I exploded. "You can't just shut off people's water without notice! Replacing a furnace isn't something that just springs on you. How hard of a job would it have been to put a notice up yesterday to let us know?"

The man stumbled over himself apologetically. "I'm very sorry, sir. I don't know why there was no notice. I'll speak to maintenance and find out why that happened."

"Well, speaking to maintenance about why it happened isn't going to get me a shower right now, *is it?* So now, I'm going to have to call and cancel my appointment, because you people can't manage a simple thing like notifying your community when you're going to turn off our water."

"I'm very sorry," he repeated. This was followed by an awkward silence.

"I have to go and—figure out how to fix this mess. So, goodbye."

I sat on the couch, seething. Should I drive up to the office in my rumpled clothes and bed head, to really make my point? I texted my next appointment: "Idiots shut off my water without notice. Have to cancel. Sorry." Then

I began to plan a letter to the CEO of the management company, expressing my outrage at the injustice.

OK. Stop.

Isn't this how we get? It doesn't seem any silver lining was found here. Yes, the circumstances were inconvenient. Yes, the management should have had more foresight. But my reaction is still my choice.

I'm pleased to inform you that, while the initiating circumstances were true, my reaction in the above account was completely fabricated. This is how it really went down.

I woke up one morning this week and went to take a shower. When I turned on the water, it hissed and sputtered, glugging out a pathetic amount of water. Then it just dripped, emitting a high-pitched whine.

I turned the lever off. *Hmmm.* I had an appointment at ten o'clock. I picked up the phone and dialed the management office.

"Hello. My hot water seems to be off. Do you know what's up?"

"I just got a notice on that, sir. Let me see . . ." He fumbled through some papers. "Yes, they're replacing your furnace today, sir. It shouldn't be more than two hours."

"Two hours. Yikes! I have an appointment in a half hour.   I didn't see a notice about it," I replied.

"I'm sorry about that, sir. I don't know why a notice wasn't put up."

"Well, at least they're fixing the broken heater," I said. "It's been on bypass for a week or so since the last one went, and it'll be good to have full heat and pressure back. Thanks."

"Again, I'm sorry for the inconvenience," the man

repeated.

"No problem. Not your doing. Thanks for the information. I've been around the world and seen some things. I should be able to handle a cold shower."

We laughed and then said our goodbyes.

I sniffed under my arm. Decent. Didn't need a full shower, I decided.

I grabbed my face wash, shampoo, a washcloth and a towel, and headed for the kitchen sink, which is deeper than in the bathroom. I turned on the cold water, running the washcloth under it. Really cold. It would certainly wake me up. Plus, cold water tightens the skin. Bonus.

I washed my face quickly, then bent down to put my head under the faucet. I was suddenly reminded of summers when I was a counselor at a camp at the northernmost part of Maine.

The bathrooms were rustic and kids used to get up at four and five in the morning to vie for the limited hot water. Anyone who got up after six took an ice cold shower. I was certainly wily and tenacious enough to get up before anyone else and take a long, hot shower. But I enjoyed thinking that, by taking a cold shower, I was sort of "giving" the hot water to one or two of the other kids. I loved that camp and my campers.

By now, I had rinsed the shampoo out and was toweling off my hair, smiling at the memory of individual kids I'd had over the years at that camp. I wondered where they were now.

Having skipped a full shower saved me time. I made my ten o'clock appointment in plenty of time.

You see, the circumstances didn't change. I just found

the silver lining. And that changed the events that *followed*. Where I could have begun the day stewing and clenching my jaw, my day was off to a great start.

On the Fourth of July this year, I got caught in bumper-to-bumper traffic in town. I had just gotten off the phone with my friend Chad who lives about a half hour away, and we'd decided I'd come down to watch an impromptu late-night movie. I had somehow forgotten that our town had fireworks this year. Once I was swept into the stream of cars around the rotary, I was stuck. It quickly became a virtual parking lot, and there was no escaping in either direction. I called Chad: "I'm going to be *very* late!"

Here again, I had a choice. Many people around me were already laying on horns and throwing arms in exasperation. *Silver lining*, I thought.

I looked over at the car going the opposite direction, stopped beside me. A boy of maybe six was in the back seat, twirling his pink glow necklace, smiling, oblivious to the traffic.

I put on the radio. I took out my cell and began to text encouraging notes to some of the kids I mentor. Many texted back with equally affirming thoughts. Some of the texted conversations really got ridiculous. I laughed more than once. I would say I managed to send positive notes to a dozen or more kids. They felt like they mattered. I had used the time wisely. Forty minutes had passed and I finally approached my escape route on the right—a street that would have been a three-minute trip under normal circumstances. After taking a few back roads, I got to Chad's almost an hour late. He couldn't have cared less. We watched our movie and stayed up talking after that. It was a terrific night.

It could have been a miserable one. I could have boiled with irritation in my car, being mad at the world. I could have decided that I was sick of it all by the time I reached the turnoff, and just canceled plans with my friend and drove home mad.

Traffic and plumbing issues aren't the worst things, you may argue. What about the *really* hard stuff that life throws at us. Where's the silver lining then?

I read a story once of a woman who was placed in a Nazi concentration camp for helping to hide Jews. She tells of how, in addition to the daily horrors she and her family endured there, her bunker of women had an outbreak of fleas. For many of them, this additional trial threatened to be the proverbial last straw. But this woman pointed out that, since the outbreak, the cruel guards had not come into their area and hassled or abused them, fearing that they would themselves be exposed to the fleas. It turns out that she and the other women had relative peace and freedom in their bunker, because of the infestation. She was adept at finding the silver lining.

My grandfather passed away in the spring of 2010. Twenty of us were around his bedside when he passed, one hand on him and another on my grandmother, his wife of nearly seventy years. It was surreal and somehow beautiful. I sang at the funeral. It was the hardest thing I think I've done. What good can come of death?

Through the planning and wake and services, our extended family bonded in ways we never had before. My grandparents had six children, who all have children. Our living line extends to great-great-grandchildren. There is a twenty-year age gap between my mother and her youngest sister. So, while I've seen many of my younger cousins at a family event here or there and we've been cordial, I've never really known them. My grandfather's death opened doors for us to know each other. In fact, if you read the acknowledgments, you'll have noted that the whole idea for writing this book came out of a graduation card I wrote to my much younger cousin, Dylan, with whom I connected in a new way during the circumstances around our grandfather's passing.

Silver linings are everywhere. Make it your personal challenge to find them. They will surprise you. And the world will begin to look different.

Practice positivity. Practice makes perfect.

CHAPTER 24

People vs. Problems

L ET ME TELL YOU ABOUT JERRY.

I met Jerry when I was working in an inner-city high school program. The program met in the basement of the school and was funded on a grant as an experiment. The kids in the program were teens on parole or probation, or who were in gangs, or who were students otherwise at high risk for truancy. The aim of the program was to find ways to keep them in school.

My first day on site, I pored over files, choosing out my first students. My goal was to identify and connect with those I felt were at critical risk level from among the already high-risk population. Jerry was a clear frontrunner.

Jerry was 17. They'd told him he was a junior; but as far as actual credits, he was only in high school because of his age and the special nature of the program. Jerry was on a strict, court-ordered probation for a number of crimes. He had already done time. One of the stipulations of his probation—the only thing preventing him from going immediately back to lock-up—was that he attend school daily. He was to obey the rules. He was to attend all classes assigned to him.

The problem was, Jerry could not read.

Jerry's file showed that he had received years of state-funded special services in reading and math. Yet, his last available test scores from only a few years earlier showed that he was still on a first-grade reading level. My priority with Jerry would not be counseling. It would not even be academic support, per se. My goal had to be to try to teach this near-man to read past "Do you like my little dog?"

I knew I could succeed—that *he* could succeed—if I could get him in the chair. My roster was complete. I went to meet the kids. Jerry was my first visit. I entered a classroom, where the teacher lounged with his feet up on his desk, and students looked at the pictures and stats of sports teams in daily papers strewn across tables. Heat began to rise in my chest. I hoped this was some sort of break time and not the norm. "I'm here to see Jerry," I announced.

Heads turned toward a lanky African-American boy with half-closed eyes that said at once that he trusted no one. Jerry's eyebrows raised self-consciously but his face remained a stone. He did not look toward the doorway where I stood. I felt for him immediately. "Hi, everyone. Hi, Jerry. Why don't you at least come out in the hall for a second so I can tell you *why* I'm here to see you." He pushed himself up roughly, the waist of his pants hanging just above his knees and the rest pooling about his sneakers in seeming bolts of denim. He sauntered to the door with a look of defiance, almost threatening. He still would not look at me, his eyes seeming to trace an invisible, zigzag line on the floor. Once he was outside the classroom, I quietly closed the door. Even leaning against the wall in a slouch, staring straight ahead, he towered over me.

I felt confident. Excited. I was *going* to teach this kid to read. More importantly, I was determined to help him see his own worth as a person. I had my work cut out for me.

"Hey, Jerry. I'm Erik. It's my first day. Listen— I read your file. So I know a little *about* you. But I don't know *you*. I hope I will. But right now, I want to ask you to take a risk with me. Look at it as a sort of dare."

He glanced *toward* me, though not quite at me. At least it was something. I kept going. "I want you to give me two weeks, an hour each day, to work with you on reading."

That was it. He was already shaking his head and gesturing vehemently, an acrid look on his face. "Naw, naw, naw. I'm not [expletive] going to your [expletive] retard classes, man!"

The window was closing. I had to act fast. I pushed forward. "Jerry, it won't be the same as before. I promise. Give me two weeks. Just ten days. And if you don't feel like you are reading much better by then, you can quit."

"I can *already* quit," he countered. "You can't *make* me do *nothin'*."

He started walking away down the hall. I drew in a breath, gearing for the big guns. I hated to have to use them, but I knew it was for his best. I followed him. "Jerry, your file says you are on probation and that you have to go to classes and follow the rules. If you don't come to my class, I will have to call your probation officer and tell him that you aren't following the program."

He stopped.

You could feel the air change, almost crackle. He spun on his heels to face me and looked me dead in the eyes for the first time. "A'ight. " It sounded like a question. A menacing challenge more than assent.

"Good decision," I said. "You won't be sorry. I promise." I turned and started down the L-hallway to the end, where my room was. Jerry followed. I tried to make small talk about what he liked to do outside of school or if he played basketball. He didn't reply. At least I would get him in the door.

I walked in and set my things down on a table. The room was stark, the walls made of large, yellowed cinder blocks that appeared to have been trying to pass for white at one time. The floors were badly chipped linoleum, with many tiles cracked or missing altogether. I thought to myself, *This isn't a far cry from what he had in lock-up!*

I turned around to invite Jerry to a seat. Jerry was squatting with his hands placed fingers inward on his thighs for support. His head was down, as if he were going to vomit. Then I realized what was happening. He wore his jeans low to begin with, but his boxers were now pulled down, as well. His bare thighs were visible between them and the hem of his XXL jersey. Something dropped to the floor.

Jerry was taking a dump.

Right there on my classroom floor and in front of me, Jerry was relieving himself. After leaving his last deposit, he unceremoniously hoisted his boxers back up and straightened his shirt. His face was all smug self-satisfaction. "That's what I thinka your [expletive] readin' class, *boy*!"

Now, this story could be used to illustrate a number of things I feel passionately about, and which are topics discussed elsewhere in this book. The fact that, regardless of our circumstances, we always have a choice. The benefits—and challenges—of choosing positivity over negativity. The idea that no one can *make* you mad. But here, I want to use it to talk about something else.

THE BEST ADVICE SO FAR:
Focus on the person, not the problem.

In those few seconds, I had some decisions to make...

Order your copy of **The Best Advice So Far** *today*
at

Available in:
print
e-book
& Audible audiobook

★★★★★

And watch for Erik Tyler's new release

You Always Have A Choice

coming in 2020

Made in the USA
Monee, IL
05 June 2020